BOOKS BY VIRGINIA S. EIFERT

THE BUFFALO TRACE
The Story of Abraham Lincoln's Ancestors

OUT OF THE WILDERNESS
Young Abe Lincoln Grows Up

THREE RIVERS SOUTH
A Story of Young Abe Lincoln

WITH A TASK BEFORE ME
Abraham Lincoln Leaves Springfield

NEW BIRTH OF FREEDOM
Abraham Lincoln in the White House

MISSISSIPPI CALLING

RIVER WORLD
Wildlife of the Mississippi

DELTA QUEEN
The Story of a Steamboat

DELTA QUEEN

The Story of a Steamboat

BY VIRGINIA S. EIFERT

Illustrated by Manning de V. Lee

1960

DODD, MEAD & COMPANY   NEW YORK

Library of Congress Catalog Card Number: 60-7034
Printed in the United States of America
by Vail-Ballou Press, Inc., Binghamton, N. Y.

This book is for Larry,
who traveled the rivers with me
aboard the DELTA QUEEN

Acknowledgments

From river, to boat, to library, to river again, doors have been opened to me so that, through direct experience, through reading and through stories told to me, I found the fabric for this book.

Most of all I am indebted to the steamboat *Delta Queen,* the heroine of the story, and to Edwin J. Quinby, Jack Quinby, and Richard Simonton, who saved her in her moment of greatest need. To Mrs. Letha Cavendish Greene, Mary Greene Cleary, Howard Nadel and the new owners, my thanks for opportunities made for me to ride the *Queen.*

To the crew and staff of the *Delta Queen* I owe much, not only for information freely given but for enduring friendships—to Captain Paul Underwood, Captain Albert Kelly, Captain Eugene Hampton and the late Captain Harry Fitzgerald; to Robert McCann, Fred Barrows, Clarke Hawley, Marty Stouder, Happy Briscoe, Harmon Mize and Bruce Edgington.

I could not have compiled much of my material without the invaluable items found in the pages of *Waterways Journal,* and the assistance of James V. Swift of that staff; or without Captain Frederick Way, Jr., and his original compilation of the *Delta Queen* material which appeared in his book, *The Saga of the Delta Queen,* from which he gave me permission to quote for my own purposes.

For many river experiences and information, I am also indebted to the late R. H. Huffmann and to Kenneth Baker of J. D. Streett and Company of St. Louis, and to the crews of the Streett towboats, on which I was permitted to ride as a guest, the *St. Louis Zephyr* and the *Cape Zephyr*.

My thanks go to Mr. and Mrs. William Leyhe of St. Louis for information on the *Golden Eagle;* to Captain Roy Barkhau for his material on the Eagle Packet Company, and to Mrs. Wilbur Finger for a firsthand account and photographs of the dramatic sinking of the *Golden Eagle.* To Mrs. Dorothy Powers of the Inland Rivers Room of the Cincinnati Public Library, my cordial thanks for Greene Line material and for a chance to read the priceless log of the *Delta Queen's* sea voyage; and to Mr. and Mrs. Howard Uible of Cincinnati, Mr. and Mrs. Frank Freeman, Vidalia, Louisiana, and Mrs. John A. Lala of New Orleans for their help along the way.

There are many more—all those who, down through the years, have known or loved or written or told of steamboats on the western rivers. Their touch is in these pages, too, enwrapped in the whole, inescapably part of it, for the story of the steamboats and the *Delta Queen* has been told in the adventures and in the lives of many people over a century and a half of river travel in mid-America.

Virginia S. Eifert

Contents

Introduction

This is the story of the last overnight passenger steamboat on the Mississippi and the Ohio. The *Delta Queen* is a vessel which has had adventures unknown to any other steamboat in all the long history of these romantic craft on the rivers of America. She is much beloved by all who know her or who see her passing by, paddle wheel churning muddy water into white foam, bound for a distant port. She is something out of the past which, by all rights, should have vanished long ago when the Steamboat Era died.

This is also the story of that lost Steamboat Era and about how the *Delta Queen* came along as the last in an unbroken line. The tale begins with the invention of a small, ineffectual steamboat in 1811, America's early attempt to bring two-way travel to the powerful currents of her one-way inland rivers.

There follows the account of the thousands of wonderful, graceful, yet often ugly and frequently dangerous vessels which created the Steamboat Era, and of how times changed —and changed—and changed, until only one remained to carry passengers in the old manner on the rivers.

There is nothing else left that is like her, no other boat to compare with the big, beautiful, strangely fateful, history-making *Delta Queen*. After you have read about the steamboats which came before her, hurry down to the landing where the *Delta Queen* waits and ride with her down two great rivers in the springtime of the year.

1. Steamboat Coming!

The hot June night along the Mississippi resounded with crickets and clattered with katydids. Lowlands were bright with the drifting sparks of fireflies; bullfrogs bellowed from backwaters; and the shrill buzzing of river-bottom mosquitoes was punctuated now and again by slapping sounds. On the dark, mud-clotted riverbanks in Tennessee and Arkansas, an uncommonly large number of people had gathered, and here and there they had built bonfires, partly for illumination, friendliness and celebration, partly to keep the mosquitoes at bay. For miles along the Lower Mississippi that night the banks were lit, and people stood or sat about, waiting, waiting. . . .

Against the dark sky far downstream they could make out a dim red glow moving along, a glow as of flying sparks against black smoke, though the chimneys which made it were invisible. Some distance away moved another glow, more sparks flaring in the night. There was a faint sound of distant cheering, the low-throated tone of a steamboat whistle, a rumbling which someone was certain came from steamboat engines.

But that was all they knew. Two steamboats were coming upstream, but which was ahead and which behind, and how far separated they were, no one could tell. In the dark, willow-grown bends of the Mississippi, who could be sure?

The postman himself that day had brought the news to the villages and farms, and the telegraph had flashed the message to towns big enough to have telegraph stations. The *Natchez* and the *Robert E. Lee,* two of the finest boats on the Mississippi, were racing at last. Old Tom Leathers had finally challenged cocky John Cannon to a race, and on a sticky-hot June night in 1870, the rival steamboats with their angry, rival captains were rapidly coming upriver to set a record between New Orleans and St. Louis.

The postman had said the *Lee* was leading, but that was because Captain Cannon had pulled out ahead of time. Still, there were no rules in a steamboat race. The Mississippi itself usually contrived to even things up after a bit, once a vessel was committed to its not always gentle care, and the river had many tricks to throw in the way of racers. Perhaps even now, people were saying, the beautiful *Natchez* had surged ahead, but no one upriver would know the truth until the racing boats flashed past.

And they were coming. The red glares were closer, brighter. The sounds of thudding pistons and grinding paddle wheels and the coughing of the exhausts were plainly heard. The low, powerful bellow of a steamboat whistle was identified as the deep-throated bumblebee voice of the *Natchez.* A defiant five-toned one must be the *Lee*—and still no one could tell which boat was ahead or likely to win the wonderful race.

The watchers, wondering and wagering and slapping mosquitoes, felt that this race, somehow, was much more than a contest between two boats. There had been a lot of river races in the past and records broken. Captain Leathers's *Princess*, in 1856, had in fact broken all records for time between New Orleans and Natchez. He had claimed the golden antlers of speed which still hung arrogantly on his wharfboat at Natchez, Mississippi, waiting to be taken by some faster boat. None had done so; there were no faster boats. Or were there? If the *Robert E. Lee* won this contest, then Captain Leathers would suffer a double grief in losing both the precious antlers and the supremacy of the *Natchez*.

This race was different because it was not only a test between two boats but a conflict between two men. The captains were enemies. Duels with swords or pistols had been outlawed for settling personal hatred, but two steamboats could prove the power of their owners, or could be blown up or sunk in trying: there was no law against it. Big, red-haired Captain Thomas Leathers of the *Natchez* and stocky, black-bearded Captain John Cannon of the *Robert E. Lee* would find out now and for all time which of the two splendid, speedy vessels and which skillful, canny captain was fastest and best on the river. But everyone who knew the men understood that, no matter what the outcome of this race might be, the two could never be friends.

Both vessels and both men were about evenly matched. The *Natchez* was 301 feet long, a slender boat, shallow draft, painted white; she was two decks high, with white railings and a fine pilothouse up on the texas deck. Her two tall, bright red chimneys were crowned with square collars bearing her name, topped with flaring iron feathers. Her pair of side-wheels, covered with a circular boxing, spun fast. She was admired and loved, while Captain Leathers, with his crisp, ruddy hair and beard and his crackling temper, his personal charm and his command of river epithets, was admired, too. His crew affectionately called him "Pushmataha," after the valiant Choctaw chieftain who helped save the southern white people from annihilation; but he was "Old Push" for short. All who knew him felt that it was far better to have Tom Leathers for a friend than as an enemy.

His bitterest enemy was Captain John Cannon whose boat, the *Robert E. Lee* was a foot shorter than the *Natchez*, but otherwise was evenly matched in size, style and speed. Her chimneys were tall and black and had white flaring feathers. She had been built in 1866, when the War Between the States was over. The war itself had done nothing to cement friendly relationships between the two men, although they had disliked each other even before that and had actually had a fistfight in a saloon brawl in New Orleans.

In his dislike of Captain Cannon and his envy of the speedy *Lee*, which was always threatening his own boat's supremacy on the river, Captain Leathers would have done almost anything to win a race, yet his sense of honor insisted that he must do it fairly and with no undue danger to passengers and freight. Captain Cannon was a more reckless man, who dared more with his boat. Some people were afraid to ride on the *Lee*, but others rejoiced in the sense of adventure they knew as soon as they stepped aboard.

Both men were Kentuckians. Both had been Confederates in the War Between the States. But Captain Leathers hated Captain Cannon's part in the war, while he himself had turned over to the Confederate forces his fifth *Natchez* and had seen her burned by the Union Army. It was then that he vowed that the flag of the United States would never fly from any boat of his. The sixth *Natchez*, racing up the river on that exciting night in 1870, bore no flag.

Captain Cannon, however, during the early portion of the war, when the Mississippi was blockaded, had taken his fine big boat, the *General Quitman,* up the Red River to Shreveport, to be out of the way of conflict until the Mississippi was opened to traffic again. When this finally took place, after the fall of Vicksburg in 1863, canny Captain Cannon set forth again on the *General Quitman,* now loaded to the guards with cotton.

For while he had waited he had purchased great quantities of cotton from isolated towns and plantations up the Red River—and he had bought exceedingly cheap. The *General Quitman* paddled down the Red and into the Mississippi and up to St. Louis, where the cargo was sold for a tremendous price. From his war profits, Captain Cannon could easily afford to pay $230,000 to build a fine boat like the *Lee.*

The boat was built at New Albany, Indiana, where the painters refused outright to letter the name-boards. New Albany had been northern in sympathy during the war, and to paint the hated name of the general who had led the South against the North in four bloody years of battle was too much to ask. So Captain Cannon, in a huff, took his name-boards over to Kentucky, where they were lettered and painted with no bother. No one, after that, seemed to object to the name of the steamboat which was making such a reputation for herself in speed, dash and popularity. The *Lee* had proved that she was almost as fast as the famous *Natchez.* But was she faster? Or only second best? The owners of the boats had to know.

Captain Leathers thereupon had challenged Captain Cannon to a race. Cannon refused. Both men had put announcements in the New Orleans papers, stating they did not contemplate the dangerous sport of racing; passengers need not hesitate to book passage. The *Robert E. Lee* and the *Natchez* would carry freight and passengers and make the usual stops from

New Orleans to St. Louis, leaving at 5 P.M. on June 30, 1870.
Nevertheless, just about everyone knew that a magnificent
race was brewing. They were even more sure of it when they
caught a glimpse of the *Lee* down at the crowded New Orleans waterfront, where steamboats were lined up for nearly
six miles. The *Lee* had been stripped of all extras, decorations,
freight, even window panes and doors. It was belatedly announced that she would carry passengers but no freight, and
there would be no stops except at Cairo and St. Louis. Passengers must stay aboard for the whole trip and, at the same time,
take part in a race for supremacy on the river.

Captain Cannon was evidently ready for a contest, but
Captain Leathers, the challenger, stubbornly let it be known
that the *Natchez* would indeed make all her usual stops and
would carry a full load of freight and passengers. He still insisted it was *not* a race. But everyone knew it was.

News got around. The New Orleans waterfront was
jammed with people that hot, dusty day and bets were being
made. Ninety passengers came aboard the *Natchez;* seventy
on the *Lee*. Suddenly, at 4:56 P.M., four minutes before the
announced departure time, Captain Cannon ordered lines
thrown off. He hastily backed the *Robert E. Lee* into the
Mississippi.

The *Natchez*, several spaces down the line-up of steamers,
could not get out until the *Lee* had finished backing and had
started forward, and then the tremendous wash and churning
water from her sidewheels provided a rough tumult that
badly hindered the laboring *Natchez* and her furious captain.
The race had indeed begun. All the way up the river for
more than a thousand miles people gathered on levees and
waterfronts and riverbanks to cheer and speculate, for this
was one of the most exciting things to have happened along
the old river since the war.

The *Robert E. Lee* maintained her lead. Only once did the

pursuing *Natchez* come close—was in fact only four hundred yards in the rear, wallowing in the muddy waves of the *Lee's* violent backwash. The *Lee* occupied the channel; the river was too low and shallow elsewhere for the *Natchez* to risk making a wide berth around the *Lee's* wheel wash. But the *Natchez* could never manage to surge ahead. Not only must she lose time in unloading passengers at the promised way points, but she developed mechanical trouble. A cold-water pump had a broken valve and water poured out, lowering steam pressure. To neglect the break invited disaster. Leathers groaned and berated his luck, but he ordered the *Natchez* to shore where, for half an hour, she was tied to a willow while fast, skillful hands repaired the break and Captain Leathers paced. He watched the smoke of the *Lee* vanish around a bend.

The *Natchez* was quickly on her way again but, in her hurry, she ran hard aground on a sand bar. The river's lowness had put shoals and bars and shallows where an incautious steamboat would scrape and stick. The *Natchez* was in such a great hurry to be on her way that she no sooner got off one sand bar before she had rammed herself on an island. It was maddening to the captain, crew and passengers.

There were further delays in refueling from waiting coal barges. The *Robert E. Lee* was managing this chore more efficiently. Captain Cannon had arranged beforehand that she would run between a pair of coal barges, which were quickly tied fast to her guards. While the steamer proceeded on her way with no loss of time, roustabouts hastily unloaded the coal, untied the barges and let them drift back to their home port. But the *Natchez* came to a full stop for loading her fuel.

The *Lee* had also secretly taken on a load of fat wood and pine knots for a hot, fast fire and extra speed. She met a steamer hidden near an island, took on her supply of emergency fuel, and was quickly on her way. But not all went well

*The race had indeed begun. All the way up the river for more
than a thousand miles people gathered on levees and waterfronts and riverbanks to cheer and speculate.*

with the *Robert E. Lee*. Like the *Natchez*, she, too, had anxieties in the engine room.

There was serious trouble with a weakened boiler. It was the same kind of break—and discovered at about the same area in the river—that had caused the big *Sultana* to blow up and burn, in 1865. Captain Cannon, tight-lipped and quiet, ordered repairs, fast; but he knew and the engine crew knew that that boiler was far from safe, might blow up anyway, in spite of the repair. And still the *Robert E. Lee* pounded ahead in the lead.

Then, just above Cairo and the mouth of the Ohio River, both boats ran headlong into thick fog.

This was too much for harassed Captain Thomas Leathers to endure. He had gone without sleep for two nights and was almost worn out with the strain. He decided not to risk the lives of his ninety passengers and crew in the dangerous Graveyard Stretch, lying menacingly enveloped in fog between

Cairo and St. Louis. He was only 180 miles from his goal, from possible success and immortality; but he was afraid to try it in the murk, even if the *Lee* should boldly attempt to do so. He could not honestly see how it would be possible.

Ahead lay the danger of Tower Rock, and all the shallows, rocks and shoals of that risky length of river. So the *Natchez* was tied to the bank, and the weary passengers and most of the crew slept. It was no use now, the captain knew; the race was lost. He just would not endanger his people further. . . . Still, there was the faint chance that, not far away in the fog, the *Robert E. Lee* was also tied up. . . . If so, what would happen when the fog lifted and again the two rivals set out?

The *Robert E. Lee* had headed boldly into the fog, then slowed to a crawl. The stuff was thick and cottony; visibility was reduced to almost nothing, yet Captain John Cannon recklessly refused to stop. A small boat with the leadsmen went ahead, slowly, slowly, sounding the way, while all the river experts on the *Lee* were stationed on the decks, to watch and listen for danger in the thick murk as the boat inched upriver. The *Lee* crept and poked and probed and nudged and backed and went forward all that night, while the *Natchez*, a few miles away, was prudently tied up to the bank for six hours. The *Lee* bluffed her way through—and she made it! As morning came, she was suddenly out of the fog and, picking up speed, charged triumphantly toward St. Louis.

The St. Louis waterfront had been crowded during most of the night. As the *Robert E. Lee* came into sight, with the *Natchez* nowhere in view, a wild roar of welcome rose from the thousands of watchers, mingled with cannon shots, blasts from all the steamboat whistles in the harbor, the ringing of bells and a long shout from the whistle of the *Robert E. Lee* herself. The *Lee* had broken all records on the river, had made the trip in three days, eighteen hours and fourteen minutes.

The actual time of the race put the *Natchez* very definitely in second place. She made it in four days and ten minutes. Yet, as furious Captain Leathers argued and would continue to argue for the rest of his life—and his friends and admirers after him—if one subtracted his time tied up and his time for repairs, and for putting off passengers and freight, and for groundings, *he* would actually have come in ahead of the arrogant *Robert E. Lee.*

But as far as the nation was concerned, the *Robert E. Lee* had won the race, and there was no doubt about it. After the golden antlers of speed were bestowed on the wonderful boat, her passenger lists were always filled until, a few years later, when financial reverses hit the *Lee*, she was retired, stripped, and ignominiously became a wharf boat at Memphis. Yet no boat in the history of the Mississippi bettered the record of the *Robert E. Lee*—at least none has ever done so yet.

2. Steam for the Western Rivers

There has been nothing else in the world quite like a
Mississippi River steamboat. While other countries and other
parts of America had steam navigation, none had the problems found on the inland rivers, known as the western rivers
of the United States.

In the Mississippi steamboat, the problems were well solved.
Within a few years after its invention, there were twice as
many of these craft hauling thousands of tons more freight
and passengers on the western rivers than there were vessels
on the Atlantic coast, on the Great Lakes, or on the Hudson
River itself, where the first steamboat had been operated.

Men had been experimenting with steam for a long time. In
fact, a steam engine was constructed in Greece's Alexandria
in the second century B.C. It was used to open the heavy
doors of a temple. There was cautious experimentation with

the tantalizing and often painful power of steam for hundreds of years after that, but not until 1698 was the first real steam engine built, a curiosity, not a structure which might alter man's pattern of transportation and civilization.

In 1760, in England, James Watt, inspired in his youth, so the story goes, by watching steam push and jiggle the lid of his mother's teakettle, invented a low-pressure condensing engine which was used by John Fitch, James Rumsey, and John Stevens in America in making a boat travel by means of a churning paddle wheel, though not very well.

John Fitch made a fairly successful steamboat in 1790. It worked, with few breakdowns and delays, at two to three miles an hour, on the Delaware, but no one had any confidence in such a contraption. The invention languished, and so did John Fitch; he died without the recognition or fame which were rightfully his.

Oliver Evans believed in steam engines, too. He developed his own, a high-pressure engine in which live steam pushed a piston in a cylinder. This moved connecting rods and cogs, to make a wheel go around.

There it was, simply (though it was not simple at all) cold water pumped up from the river . . . converted into steam in a boiler heated by a furnace . . . forced through pipes to a cylinder in which a piston was thrust up and down . . . the piston connected with a shaft to an axle of a wheel set with wooden planks . . . *and a boat moved through the water!* It required a good many improvements and additions to keep it running, to give push and power, but essentially, this was it.

But it took Robert Fulton in New York State to put together in one model the most usable parts of other men's inventions. In 1807, the *North River Steamboat of Clermont* turned its sidewheels on the Hudson River and carried delighted, if somewhat uneasy, passengers. Her furnace burned oak wood, and her Boult and Watt engine throbbed so hard that the whole vessel quivered. And, just in case the engine failed, there were masts and sails in readiness.

The *Clermont* was not exactly a small craft. She was 140 feet long, slender and sleek-lined, and she had a keel, though not a deep one. Robert Fulton and his associates were pleased with the success of the steamboat and built several others. Then the group cast about for other areas needing this form of transportation and easily found the best place of all—the Ohio and Mississippi River system.

These rivers, attracting as they were a growing number of people who were seeking homes beyond the Alleghenies, were waterways that needed steamboats. There was, in fact, hardly any other place in America where steamboat travel was more desperately needed just then.

One of Fulton's partners, Nicholas Roosevelt, and his wife, an intrepid woman who refused to be left at home when her husband was doing exciting things, went out to the Ohio and traveled by raft, taking soundings down to the Mississippi. After that, Roosevelt was certain that the regular Fulton-type steamboat was not going to work satisfactorily on these great rivers, so unlike the Hudson, but no one listened to him.

He had discovered that the Ohio and the Mississippi were most unreliable waters. They were not like the Hudson and the Delaware. One never knew what the western rivers would do or be like from one day to the next or from one hour to the next, while even their courses might be totally changed by the next year. Water levels could rise fast to flood stage over night; they could drop almost as quickly and leave monstrous sand bars and shoals standing up like cliffs from the river bottom, with only a precarious channel winding between them. A usable steamboat must be able to navigate low water as well as high, land anywhere and travel over thousands of miles in what was then untamed, unmarked wilderness.

One of the great advantages, however, Roosevelt pointed out, was the fact that these rivers traversed great forests. Difficult as the watercourses might be, there would at least never be any lack of firewood to feed the furnaces which boiled the water for the steam engines, which would, therefore, be able to turn the paddles of any number of steamboats!

Before steamboats ventured on these furious streams, the sole craft had been canoes, flatboats, rafts and keelboats. However, most of their journeys were one-way. Canoes could come back, but the route was hard. Keelboats could do it, too, but the method was even harder. It often meant that brawny members of the crew literally pulled the boat up the Mississippi, as they trudged through underbrush and mud on shore, or poled their way laboriously upstream. But the big rafts and flatboats that were loaded with people and produce could never come back up those rivers.

In spite of all that rough country along the Mississippi and the Ohio, people were settling out there. They were building their villages and towns and farms close to the rivers, so that they could use them for transportation, for in that Middle Western wilderness there were hardly any roads. The markets were often more than a thousand miles away from where meat, grain, furs and lumber were produced. A workable steamboat would bring these things quickly to market and people to towns; would bring civilization to the central portion of America. It was the single boon most needed along the great, wild Mississippi Valley.

So the Fulton interests built the first steamboat for the Mississippi at Pittsburgh, in 1811, and named her the *New Orleans*. She was pretty, and she was painted blue—almost every other river steamer after that, however, was painted white—and she made a great fuss churning down the river. She startled and alarmed the Chickasaws, found herself involved in the disastrous earthquake of 1811 and contrived to make just one hair-raising, horrifying journey to New Orleans, her namesake city, for, after all that tribulation and effort, the little steamboat could not get back. Her engines were too feeble to carry her up the powerful river, and her deep keel was impossible in shallow water.

Soon after the *New Orleans* and several succeeding steamboats failed to get back up the river, Captain Henry Shreve invented the first really workable Mississippi River steamboat. He had navigated the Fulton-type boats and decided that he knew what was the matter with them. They were still patterned very much on the lines of ocean ships, deep-water vessels; they just did not fit the Mississippi and the Ohio.

Henry Shreve built the *Washington*. She was very much like a flat barge, with her engines on the deck level rather than in a hold. She had passenger cabins on a deck above, the pilothouse on top of that. River men were amused. They called Henry Shreve a fool to think that such an impossible craft would be able to navigate, much less stay upright in a wind.

But the *Washington* went down to New Orleans and then came back in such quick time that everyone along the rivers was full of tremendous excitement. This was what they had been waiting for—fast transportation between those widely separated river ports. The *Washington* had had her troubles, but her wise captain noted what was wrong, and the later boats which he built were highly successful. They and all the steamboats which came to the western rivers followed the design Shreve had worked out—"a raft with about $11,000 worth of engines and jigsaw work on it!" as many people said.

For a long time, this was a fairly good description of a steamboat. Following Henry Shreve's plan for keeping the hull of a river vessel as shallow and flat as possible, with only the suggestion of a keel, the engines were put on the lower deck. Boilers, surrounded by furnaces, pipes, and the big

shafts connecting with the paddle wheel or wheels, occupied this deck, along with freight, cotton bales—and the passengers who had little money but a desire or need to travel. Above this rose a second deck for the first-class passengers, with the pilothouse above this.

The paddle wheel was either fastened at the stern or located as two side-wheels a little past the middle of the vessel, toward the stern. This was, simply, a heavy axle surrounded by a frame containing planks set at an angle, called bucket planks. These whacked the water as the wheel was turned by the crankshafts and pistons. The wheel's push through the water propelled the boat. The little *Washington* had a wheel eight by twelve feet, but as steamboats grew in size, so did the wheels, until some were forty feet high and forty feet wide.

When the increased size of the wheel made it difficult to support one at the stern, side-wheels covered with boxing seemed more practical. On the outside of this casing the name of the vessel was usually inscribed in fancy lettering, often with flourishes, sunsets, Columbias, stags, flags, crags, or other scenery.

Here the paddle wheels had a better foundation and helped to stabilize the boat. When each wheel had its own engine and shaft, it was possible to turn them in opposite directions, thus permitting the steamboat to pivot on its base. The side-wheeler, in fact, was considered so superior as a boat that insurance rates for a time were much higher for stern-wheel boats. Some insurance companies even refused to take risks on these supposedly unreliable craft.

But accidents happened to side-wheelers, too. They were often made helpless in strong head winds, were frequently disabled by ice or heavy drift coming head on at the boat. On the other hand, many pilots preferred the stern-wheel packet because it could operate on the narrow, shallow rivers, could carry more cargo because less room was taken by the pair of side-wheels, could turn and maneuver easily, and it went faster.

Thrusting out from the bow of the steamboat was the landing stage—sometimes two of them. While the vessel was in motion, the stage was held up at an angle, to be out of the way, then it was lowered to the shore during a landing. Because of the unstable condition of the shores and water levels, there were few permanent docks or wharves along the Mississippi or the lower Ohio. Cities often had a wharf boat—an old steamboat or barge converted into a floating shed and tied to the bank so that the wharf boat could rise or fall with high or low water. Here a steamboat could pull in parallel to the wharf boat and discharge passengers and freight with ease, but it had to pay a fee for the privilege.

Elsewhere, the adjustable landing stage, as much a signature of a steamboat as the paddle wheel, solved the problem of landing. The boat headed toward the soft mud shore and nosed in, the wheel turning just enough to hold it there, while the stage, a narrow portable bridge with a hand rail, was let down until its far end rested solidly on the ground. Thus, a steamboat could halt easily almost anywhere, to take on or discharge passengers. The big boats, however, usually had regular stops at towns and seldom indulged in bank landings. Vessels with a regular schedule were known as packet boats, the speed-queens of the rivers.

The boat's decks rose in layers, each with its separate uses and inhabitants. Supported by posts above the open first deck, with its stage, engines, machinery, paddle wheel, freight and impoverished passengers, rested the boiler deck. Although no boiler was ever known to be on that second level, the name persisted. This was where the first-class passengers slept and ate and promenaded, drank, gambled, talked . . . and whiled away the time on a long river journey.

The gentlemen's cabin was forward, the ladies' cabin aft because, it was said with true chivalry, a boat most often blew up at the forward end, and it was better for the men to take the risks! There were bunks along the walls of the long cabins, given privacy by curtains. By day, the gentlemen's cabin was set with long tables on which the often elaborate meals were served by white-coated Negroes. Later in steamboat history, as vessels grew more comfortable, the long cabins were divided into small staterooms, all facing on the outer promenades around the deck, with doors leading to an inner hall running the length of the deck. The latter was the dining salon.

Above the boiler deck and passengers' quarters was the pilothouse, with its wheel for steering, its bells and speaking tube to the engine room, its spittoon, chairs, charts, a bench for visiting pilots, and a stove in winter. Back of the pilothouse was the texas deck, which originally provided sleeping space for the officers. Later, this was used for some of the passengers as well, and when the pilothouse was placed on top of the texas, on the hurricane roof, the entire texas deck was devoted to staterooms.

And rising majestically from the furnaces, straight up through the whole boat, were the chimneys, usually two, though on occasion there was but one. Two chimneys—and as the boats grew larger and taller, so did the stacks through which poured black smoke and flying red sparks. The escape pipes let off extra steam, with a deep-throated, hoarse chuffing sound.

Chimneys soon developed style. Most of them were decorated at the top with recurved iron feathers or petals, in a sort of Neptune's crown of great elegance. They grew so tall—on at least one great boat the chimneys stood seventy-five feet above the water—that they had to be supported and strengthened by guy wires. Between the chimneys were hung the deer antlers which were the prize for speed; or a golden ball, a cotton bale, or a large iron monogram of the company.

Thus the steamboat as we know it evolved, layer by layer, deck by deck. When a fine, big, white steamer, blazing with lights and casting shimmering reflections in the black water, passed by in the night, it was one of the loveliest and most exciting sights in all the dark wilderness along America's watercourses.

3. Hoodoos and Dragon Boats

Something terrible, the Mandan runner gasped, was coming up the river! Something strange and supernatural was moving along the yellow waters and among the sand bars of the Missouri! The Indian runner threw himself down on the stony ground to get his breath again, while another Mandan set off with the message. Along the valley of the Missouri the word had passed—among Pawnee and Ponca, among Assiniboin and Blackfoot and Cree. An unknown monster, breathing smoke from its nostrils, was on its way upstream. And if any tribesman had ever seen a steamboat before, he would not have recognized it as the thing which coughed and paddled and snorted and paused and advanced upon the uncertain waters of the wild Missouri.

When Major Stephen H. Long was commissioned to conduct a troop of United States soldiers and a group of scientists and map makers into the unknown land west of the Mississippi he was unsure of the attitude the Indians would take. Ever since Napoleon had sold the Louisiana Territory to President Jefferson, in 1803, expeditions had been going westward, to try to discover what lay out there in all those vast distances, behind those imposing mountains, and to find out how far away lay the Pacific Ocean.

To travel straight west was to court death. Foot travel was precarious, at best; and, once the heat, drouth and menace of the Great Plains were overcome, there were the Rocky Mountains to cross. Beyond them lay desert, and no one was sure how many more awful miles had to be traversed and conquered before, at last, the pioneers discovered the sea. Just as the Ohio and the Mississippi had been the highways to the discovery of the middle reaches of America and the Gulf of Mexico, so now did the course of the Missouri lead men to find the Pacific.

In 1805, Lewis and Clark had led a daring expedition, with the invaluable help of a young Indian woman named Sacajawea. They traveled by small boats up the Missouri to its headwaters, and then portaged a short way over the mountains to the headwaters of the Columbia River, which took them dramatically to the sea. Lewis and Clark had carefully noted new birds, animals and plants which they discovered along the way. Clark's nutcracker, Lewis's woodpecker, a flower called Clarkia and another called Lewisia are some which remind us of the expedition.

But the land out there was too great for a few men to encompass adequately with any degree of thoroughness. After the Lewis and Clark expedition returned with news of its discoveries, other groups were sent out. Shortly after young Lieutenant Zebulon Pike came back from his search for the source of the Mississippi, in 1806, he followed the Arkansas River west to the Rocky Mountains. And in 1819, Major

Stephen H. Long's party set out with a great supply of scientific instruments and collecting equipment, to check on what lay in the land of the Yellowstone. The monumental tales of the frontiersman, Jim Bridger, about what was out there— boiling springs, great waterfalls, shooting geysers, colored mud—had to be verified.

Reports concerning the Indians in the Yellowstone country indicated that they were generally hostile. No one knew how they would accept a coughing, churning, smoke-belching steamboat, but the government had commissioned a small one named the *Western Engineer* for the use of the Long expedition, as far as navigable water could be found.

Steamboats were still new and untried on the western rivers. It was, in fact, only eight years since the little *New Orleans* had battled the earthquake and was fired on by furious Chickasaws, hidden along the shores of the Ohio. Indians had resented the monster churning up their stream. They protested that the thing's smoke would wither cornfields and destroy the forest, that the pounding paddle wheel would kill all the fish.

Although other steamboats following the *New Orleans* had run into little trouble with Indians, everyone knew that the land beyond the Mississippi was untamed and that the Indians out there had known little of the settling influence of white civilization. To send a small, defenceless little steamboat with weak engines up the unknown Missouri seemed foolhardy.

But the Indians were superstitious; everyone knew that. They had many legends of monsters and dragons, like the fabulous Piasa Bird whose picture had been painted on a cliff beside the Mississippi River. If they were afraid of dragons, then why not disguise the little *Western Engineer* as one?

A grotesque figure of a serpentlike monster was built quite around and over the vessel. In an artist's sketch made of the *Western Engineer* before the departure of the expedition, the creature's body passed gracefully over the boxing of the side-wheels, while the sinuous neck ended in a great head through whose open nostrils the exhaust steam snorted forth in a most realistic and startling manner.

News went ahead as the little vessel left St. Louis and fol-lowed the powerful, yellow mud-water of the Missouri. Now and again, a group of Pawnee horsemen stood silhouetted on a butte, watching. Or a wondering Mandan hunter crouched behind a thicket of young cottonwoods or rabbit brush until the thing had passed. But the *Western Engineer* paddled and coughed and snorted and puffed, with little difficulty, through the villages of the Indians along the Missouri. Whether the people were actually afraid or if they were sim-ply amazed at this apparition on the river, the dragon boat's disguise may have been of some use.

It was the Missouri mud, not the Indians, which caused the most trouble for the *Western Engineer*. Missouri River mud is thick and colorful, coming as it does from the paint country of the Yellowstone and the rainbow buttes of Montana. Mud was bad enough in the Mississippi, but in the Missouri it was worse. It quickly settled in the boilers and clogged the valves, cutting down on steam and power. The boilers had to be cleaned out every fifteen hours or less, and this meant stop-ping the boat and unbolting the cooled boilers, so that a man could go inside and shovel out the sediment.

Not a man on the crew relished this job. Since this prom-ised to be a long trip, and it looked as if certain individuals would be spending a large part of it in cleaning mud out of boilers, one man figured a way to simplify the task. He rigged up a valve through which the mud could be blown out. It was a simple invention but a wonderful one for steamboats, because it led the way to the invention of the mud drum, from which sediment could be easily removed—mud, deadly enemy of river craft.

In spite of such commonplace yet serious troubles as mud, the story of the steamboats is a saga of drama and disaster, of elegance and envy. They aided in conquering the western wilderness and in settling the river valleys. They provided a means of traveling through jungly or swampy forests and over prairie distances where there were no real roads, few towns and little civilization.

The Steamboat Era lay mostly between 1830 and 1890. In sixty years a new way of life rose in America. In that time, thousands of big and little steamboats busily worked the rivers and the small backwaters and bayous, carrying passengers and just about everything else. Steamboats loaded freight, mail, poultry and people; livestock and honeymooners; backwoodsmen and English authors; swindlers, gamblers, criminals, escaped prisoners; and soldiers, crates of eggs, kegs of kerosene, whiskey, cider, vinegar and lard; hides, hoop-poles and honey; and more tons of cotton than any other conveyance before or since. Steamboats on the Lower Mississippi were the great cotton carriers, and many a large craft was built expressly for this trade. The space between the main deck and the boiler deck was raised, in order to pack more bales in place, until all one could see was a great wall of brown bales, often nine thousand of them, with the white fluff bursting through, sandwiched between the floor of the main deck and a boiler deck which appeared to perch directly on top of the cotton itself.

At least six thousand steamboats were built and operated during the Steamboat Era. Most of them made money for their owners. Only a few boats lasted more than five years, but since, after a year's performance, most steamboats had already paid for themselves, every additional year showed profit to the owners.

Because river life was hard on craft of every kind, a steamboat was most often built for economy as well as speed. It was frequently made of flimsy wood which was elaborately painted and decorated with Victorian fretwork and jigsaw ornaments called "gingerbread," a term given to something cheap and unsubstantial placed where it really had no use or meaning.

Steamboat gingerbread may not have served any real architectural purpose, except for deceit, but it became an integral part of the picture of steamboats, and they would have seemed stark and plain without it. The canny builders knew that a lot of cut-out jigsaw art on a boat not only covered a multitude of structural faults, but actually attracted passengers.

Nearly everything but the machinery was made of wood. Iron or steel hulls did not come into use until well past the middle of the Steamboat Era. They raised the cost of construction, yet gave vessels a longer life and far more assurance of safety than any of the wood-hulled sort. The engines and machinery were made of iron and brass and steel. They were usually well built and sturdy.

The engines were usually salvaged and put on a new boat when a vessel containing them went to its reward at the bottom of the river or on a sand bar and could not be raised or reconditioned. Sometimes the machinery outlasted half a dozen boats. Though it was frequently done, it was not considered wise to transfer the boilers from one steamer to another. The lifetime of one boat was about the lifetime of a boiler, and over-use usually resulted in an explosion.

There also was the sentimental, if thrifty, custom among many rivermen to transfer the bells and whistles of a wrecked or dismantled steamer to another boat, as if thus, in some measure, they were preserving the spirit of the dead craft. The excursion steamer *Avalon*, still actively operating out of Cincinnati, possesses a three-way whistle, put together from a trio of lost boats. The basso pipe came from a vessel which worked out of Pittsburgh soon after the beginning of the twentieth century. The baritone whistle came from the excursion steamer *America;* the soprano pipe from the excursion steamer *Princess.* The huge bell of the *Delta Queen* originally belonged to the *Queen City,* one of the biggest and finest of the more recent steamboats on the Ohio. That bell weighs 1,200 pounds and has a wonderfully sonorous, almost deafening tone and a thunderous vibration.

The steamboat *Susie B,* built in 1876, was originally used on the Lower Mississippi, but later was operated on the Suwanee River, in Florida, where her name was, naturally, changed to *Suwanee.* In 1920, the *Suwanee* sank, and, nine years later, Henry Ford had her engines salvaged and put on a boat which was built for use in Ford's Greenfield Village, near Detroit, Michigan. Here, a portion of the old channel of the Rouge River was dredged as a circular lagoon with an island in the middle, around which the reconstructed *Suwanee II* still operates with the old engines of her namesake.

This sort of transfer did not always seem to be a good idea, at least to those who were somewhat superstitious, as many river people were. There was, for example, the handsome packet *Belle Memphis*, wrecked on a sand bar below St. Louis in 1897. Her whistle was salvaged from the wreck, where it lay disintegrating on the sand bar which would later become known on the maps as the Belle of Memphis Towhead, and was put on the *Mary Morton* of the Diamond Jo Line.

Twenty-three days later, the *Mary Morton* was wrecked and sunk about twenty-five miles away from where the lost *Belle Memphis* lay gathering sand on her ruined hulk.

Many rivermen vowed that this was no more than to be expected when a steamboat was given a title having the letter M. This invariably meant bad luck and downright ruin. They could quote any number—the *Moselle*, the *Monsoon*, the *St. Martin*, the *Missouri Belle*, the *Monmouth*, the *Maria*, the *Helen McGregor*. . . . Of course, other boats were being wrecked, too. It wasn't just the M boats that were hoodooed, though an uncommonly large number of them did seem to be, at that.

But vulnerable though they were, steamboats were the life of the rivers, their daily excitement, their drama and delight. At a time when stagecoach travel was cramped, uncomfortable and unsure, and when the early railroads were little better, the space, speed and comfort of most packet boats—even if they might not be considered so favorably today—seemed all the greater and more luxurious by contrast.

People had been accustomed to associating discomfort with travel. One suffered in getting from one place to another. Travel was one of the best arguments for staying at home. But that was not always true, now, on the better steamboats. One's bed and board and comfortable chairs and agreeable companions went along on one's journeyings on the river. It was almost like staying at a fine hotel, yet traveling at the same time.

To a people from the middlewestern backwoods, riding on a river steamer was an event like nothing ever before experienced. For many, it was their first introduction to a way of life more elegant than a log cabin, and to a dinner table offering immeasurably more than the usual pioneer fare of fried pork, cornbread, hominy, or squirrel stew. A person was in a different world when he was on the river. Boys dreamed of taking the ride some day, and men saved their money so they could treat themselves and their families to this wonderful adventure.

To the awed eyes of those who rode for the first time, the magnificent structure, the white paint, the elaborate fretwork, the gilding, the oil paintings and tapestry, the glitter and illumination, the broad staircases, music, carpets, and the service of white-coated Negroes—all combined to give a dazzling impression that was like catching a glimpse of a particularly gaudy version of heaven.

Of course, this took money. Without it, the passenger didn't see much magnificence but rode below, deck class. He brought his own poke of victuals and his bundle of bedding, and tried to endure the close association of other passengers who were as uncomfortable as he, along with horses, hogs, chickens, geese, bales of cotton, smelly buffalo hides and other freight, including flies, fleas, mosquitoes and assorted vermin.

There also might be someone who was ill with cholera or yellow fever or smallpox and who, by means of the steamboat, carried the diseases to far places and among many towns.

But, for the price of a first-class fare, passengers had greater sanitation, had carpets and glassware, waiters and an elaborate menu, a magnificent salon and comfortable staterooms. The people on the boiler deck and the texas deck were hardly aware of those who rode beneath them among the freight. There were two very different worlds on the steamboat, and the inhabitants of each rarely saw the other.

These two worlds, from pilothouse to engine room, were in charge of a crew, working together, sometimes resenting each other, but all laboring to make the boat operate safely and on time. Their job was to keep the passengers happy and well fed and eager to come back; to take on freight and put off the right things at the right stops; in short, to make a profit for the company and earn their pay—and uphold the honor and dignity of the river world.

The best paid man on the boat was the pilot. He had to be an expert. He must know the river day and night, in all conditions of weather and of high and low water, upriver and down, under any circumstances. He must be able, literally, to smell danger and be capable of getting his boat out of narrow squeaks with disaster. A crack pilot could earn $750 a month, which was a great deal of money in the Steamboat Era. The captain made only about half as much, but often he was the owner of the boat. His job included coordination of the crew, keeping the passengers in a good mood, settling disputes among the help, navigating when necessary and arranging and controlling the trip. Clerks took care of receiving money for fares and assigned passengers to their staterooms, with as little argument and rearranging as possible. The "mud-clerk" was responsible for taking on and putting off freight at the proper places and keeping the business accounts straight. He was called by that name because it was his unenviable job to leap ashore as soon as the steamer touched the bank, which was often of the consistency of soft fudge and frequently immersed him in mud from ankles to knees before his business was accomplished.

The first mate directed the roustabouts in the freight handling and the routine of docking or casting off. The leadsman took soundings with a pole or lead line, to determine the river's depth in tricky stretches. The engineer, taking bell signals from the pilot, was in charge of the crew in the engine room, a group who worked in a continuous bath of steam and broiling heat—the firemen, oilers, strikers. And it was their job to keep the fires hot, the steam gauges up, the machinery working; to repair breaks without stopping the boat; often to do the best they could with equipment which might be wearing out, had been patched or precariously mended, and which might blow them and everyone else sky-high at any moment.

The engine room crew was controlled from the topmost part of the boat. Up in the pilothouse, in the exclusive haunts of the "sky parlor," the pilot in lonely glory and self-imposed isolation, with only the occasional company of other pilots, the captain or, at times, of invited guests, watched the river and turned the big, inlaid wheel—and knew that on him, and him alone, lay the real safety of the boat.

He used a system of brass bell pulls to signal changes in course to the engine room, but if he got no results or they were slow in coming, the speaking tube was used with sizzling effect. There was seldom any great affection between pilot and engine room. The latter usually called the former "Old Jingle Bells," but the epithets grew stronger during a particularly trying session of difficult navigation, when the pilot seemed to be calling for full speed ahead, full speed astern, or both at once, too fast for any man to follow. There may not have been a very friendly feeling between pilot and engineer, yet on these two lay the fate and future of the steamboat and her passengers.

But it was the passengers themselves who determined the success or failure of the steamboat. They actually loved the craft. Steamboats were the darlings of the river. A good many of them came to have personalities almost like humans, and they could be recognized from afar by the pattern of their chimneys on the sky or the particular tone and timbre of their whistles. It was not the boat crew but the passengers themselves who, one day late in the Steamboat Century, decreed that the end of steamboats had come. They turned in fickle affection to the railroads and other means of transportation, in a land which the steamboats themselves had helped to open up and civilize. A long time had passed since a dragon boat had gone snorting up the Missouri, since boatmen declared the *Moselle* blew up because its name began with the fateful M, since Henry Shreve decided that a Mississippi steamboat should be a "raft with $11,000 worth of machinery and jig-saw work" . . . a long time.

4. Death Rode the River

The big *Sultana* lay quietly at the battered, charred Vicksburg landing. She had once been an elegant boat, but now she was weary and creaked in her seams; her exhaust came gently, like a palpitating sigh, and one of her aging boilers was leaking with a steady flow which promised a worse break soon. On that April day in 1865, just about everything along the Lower Mississippi looked battered and worn and sad, and there was hardly a steamboat which was safe to use on a long trip.

Steamboats had been impressed into army service and had been given little or no care or upkeep during their years of trial and pain. With the conflict over, their paint was peeling, their boards split or broken or carved with initials. These might have been the initials of men who had died on the battlefield at Vicksburg or at Gettysburg or at Chancellorsville, or who might lie with a sunken vessel, at the bottom of the Mississippi. Men and materials were expendable, and many a once-fine steamboat had weakened or run aground or had been snagged or burned or exploded during the War Between the States, and it was all in the line of conflict and the fate of battle.

Some of the vessels had been especially built for war. A fleet of ironclads had been constructed at St. Louis, to enter the fight down the Mississippi, the Tennessee, or the Cumberland. Colonel Ellet had built a fleet of armor-clad rams. They were still steamboats, but well disguised. For want of enough government funds to build new boats, James Eads at St. Louis took a lot of passenger and freight steamers and, in desperation, set his men and shipyards to transforming them for army duty. Workmen concealed the comfortable steamboat lines with slabs of iron, buffered the magazines and engines with great coils of rope or mattresses of straw, equipped them with guns and gun turrets for fighting.

And now the war was over, had been finished for eleven days—so recently, in fact, that the scarred nation, North and South alike, could hardly believe that it was really done. April 26th and the peace terms at Appomattox itself seemed like a distant dream. The grief over Abraham Lincoln's death was still fresh across the North, rekindled at every stop of the funeral train on its long journey to Illinois.

Meanwhile, men were being released from southern prisons and returned to their homes in the North, in a huge prisoner exchange, as fast as transportation could be provided. Railroads were in a battered and broken condition after war's destruction; the easiest and only way in many cases was to send thousands of men home by steamboat. In spite of the fact that most of the steam vessels in the South, at that time, were in bad condition, unrepaired or just held together with makeshift patches, baling wire or rope, it was on some of these very boats that great numbers of feeble, long-imprisoned men were being loaded.

The *Sultana*, one of these, had been a proud, majestic vessel in the cotton trade, one of the handsomest and best known and admired on the river. Now, as more than two thousand half-starved, pitifully happy Union soldiers filed up the landing stage, the old, over-used, weakened floor boards protested the overload, and the great vessel listed until enough men had distributed themselves on both sides. Filled with eagerness and gratitude, they streamed aboard and then simply sat or lay in rows on the decks. There was really nothing else for them to do, no room for private quarters for so many. But after the horrors of the prison, just being in the open air of springtime was glorious, the April sunshine luxurious beyond belief.

The captain knew he had taken on more than a thousand too many passengers. He knew that the old *Sultana* was desperately overcrowded. He knew she had a leaking boiler and an aging mechanism which had not been inspected for a long time. Yet he watched the men come on without a protest. He was tired and disillusioned, and he really did not care.

Heavily, the *Sultana* at last set off from Vicksburg. She moved slowly against the spring current. The crew in the engine room worried about the leaking boiler. It was getting worse. The captain agreed to stop at Memphis about dusk, to have it hastily patched up, but no one examined the job afterward, to see if the work had been done properly. The *Sultana* again pushed off into the darkness of the Mississippi River, heading north from Memphis on a chill and starless April night.

Crew and officers on the gunboat *Grosbeak*, stationed in Memphis harbor, stood on their deck and watched the *Sultana* move past and out into the river. The men waved. In a little while, the lights on the *Sultana* vanished around a bend.

A few hours later, there was a sudden and tremendous roar in the distance. The noise smote on the eardrums like a giant concussion of sound, an appalling thunder of disaster. A great burst of fire leaped into the sky. An officer on the *Grosbeak* hastily used a telescope on the glare and made it out to be a large steamboat burning. There had just been time enough for the *Sultana* to have gone that far. . . .

Boats raced north, but it was too late to help very much. The weakened boiler of the old boat had exploded. Tons of steam, pieces of iron boiler, hot coals and wood of the after-deck and the bodies of hundreds of men were hurled violently into the night. The cabin and hurricane decks were torn out and so were the stairways. Flames burst out everywhere in the dry old structure. The pilot vainly tried to run the blazing ruin ashore, but the terrified passengers who remained aboard and still alive were leaping into the river, where most of them were lost.

Many of the survivors clung to barrels, window shutters, pieces of railing; some of them floated down the river as far as Memphis and were rescued. Boats coming up found some of them and pulled them to safety. But worn army caps drifted without owners, small treasures brought back from southern campaigns sank to oblivion in the Mississippi.

Many men were rescued, but 1,547 died. Until the sinking of the ocean liner, *Titanic*, in the Atlantic, in 1912, this was the greatest tally of American dead in a shipwreck. Yet, hideous as it was, not a great deal of notice was taken of the *Sultana* disaster. It came so close to the even more terrible lists of war dead which continued to pour in, to grieve the homes of North and South; came so close to that day when a stillness drew over the battlefields, and the President lay dead. At the time that the *Sultana* blew up, crowds were filing through the capitol at Albany, New York, to view the body of Abraham Lincoln, and, that same day, a gunshot ended the life of the assassin, John Wilkes Booth. A calamity like the loss of 1,547 lives in the river when an old steamboat blew up came in the shadow of so many other disasters, a compounding of human agony by war, that the people simply accepted it. In 1865, Americans had become numbed to horror.

The ruined *Sultana* was never salvaged, but lay where she sank, near Mound City, Arkansas. In the years between then and now, the Mississippi has changed its course so that the remains of the riverboat must now lie far inland, embedded in the bottomland earth of Arkansas, with perhaps a forest growing out of her grave. In 1955, the owners of the land in the approximate area of the disaster decided to begin a search for the remains of the historic steamer, but it was a futile pursuit. The *Sultana* was gone forever.

The *Sultana* was only one of many craft lost in the river. Steamboats worked hard and had a short life, for numerous and varied were the dangers to river vessels, especially wood-hulled boats which were so vulnerable to snags and sand bars, to fire and explosion. There were some durable ones, like the hardy *Virginia*, which lived for more than thirty years and survived several sinkings, snaggings and the embarrassment of being stranded in a cornfield when a flood went down. But many of the steamboats were done for in a few years after launching, their glory tarnished, carpets worn out, the woodwork broken and chipping.

Aside from high-pressure boilers in the engine room, probably the next greatest danger came from snags in the river. A snag, often called a "hull inspector"—not entirely in jest—was not always an innocuous stick of timber placidly floating in the water, able to do no more damage than to foul up a paddle wheel. A snag could be a monstrous lance fastened to the bottom of the river, with perhaps only the tip visible, or hidden entirely beneath the surface and ready to gouge out the

insides of a steamboat which rammed herself upon it like a sausage upon a fork.

Snags were originally the trees of the river forests, trees which gave way when the river ate up a shore and sent sand, earth, and vegetation into the water. Here a fallen tree was shoved about and rolled and worried until most of its twigs were broken off and only its massive trunk and limbs and iron-hard, octopus-armed roots remained. These might break up, or the whole thing might finally come to rest crosswise or at a slant in the river, the sharp end pointing straight up, aimed at navigation . . . waiting.

When steamboats began, the Mississippi was almost impassable in places where forests of snags lay in wait, until Henry Shreve used his snagboat, the amazing *Heliopolis*, to clear them out. But there was always a new crop of snags.

Less evident but still lying in wait, they remain a menace to boats today. They are the fangs of the river, the teeth of the Mississippi. One snag could ruin a fragile steamboat. When a great hole was gouged in the hull, the vessel usually sank quickly and with no advance warning—and consequent great loss of life.

Collisions were another cause of desperate accidents. Perhaps the worst of all occurred in 1837. Four hundred unhappy Creek Indians had been packed aboard the *Monmouth* during the evacuation of the southern tribes. Bowed down with grief at leaving their old homes in Tennessee and Mississippi and fearfully uncertain of their future in an unknown land, they wailed their dolorous chants or, wordless and hopeless, sat wrapped in blankets. Then, with no warning, the *Monmouth* struck a sister riverboat, the *Warren*. As she went down, no Indian escaped to find the questionable solace of a new home in a strange country. Perhaps none of them even tried.

And there were steamboat fires. It was so easy to start a a conflagration on a steamboat, almost impossible to stop it. Combustible bales of cotton and hay usually were stacked on the lower deck. Flying sparks and live embers issued from the chimneys or burst from the furnaces themselves when the firemen threw in coal or wood, scattering carelessly all around. Everything about a steamboat was so highly inflammable that, when a fire started, there usually was no stopping it until the vessel was destroyed.

All these disasters and terrors, moving ruthlessly through the entire story of steamboats in America, should have frightened people away from riding them. It was a wonder that so many continued to risk their lives on such dangerous craft when, in spite of insurance inspectors and rules, so many of them blew to Kingdom Come, or burned, or sank, or rammed on a snag or sand bar, or were crushed in ice, taking a lot of passengers with them.

Until the steamboats came along—charming, alluring, dangerous—America had known no mass killing of its people. There were plenty of single accidents, and there was war; there were Indian massacres, too, but never before had a single machine been given the power to destroy several hundred people at a time, in some of the most horrid means of perishing ever devised.

Yet people continued to ride the steamboats because they were fast, fashionable, fun and really the only comfortable way to travel. And not all of them got into trouble. Plenty of steamboats killed no one and lived to a dignified retirement as wharf boat or barge.

Much effort was put forth to remedy the dangers attendant on steamboat travel, for men knew that the Mississippi and the Ohio and the Missouri formed a vital network of waters which connected commercially important cities like Pittsburgh, Cincinnati, Louisville, and Chicago with Minneapolis, Omaha, Kansas City, New Orleans and St. Louis and, eventually, with ports of the world.

The U.S. Corps of Engineers was put in charge of river improvements, but their efforts did not pick up much momentum until after the War Between the States. Then the Mississippi River Commission and the Coast Guard accomplished much toward making the rivers safe and navigable. On steamboats, safety valves for high-pressure engines were ordered to be used. The years went by with continuous improvements to rivers and to boats—and Americans were fond of both.

But European travelers, especially authors, had a good deal to say for, about and against American steamboats, although these critical visitors never refrained from using this scorned means of transportation to get about in the awkwardly enormous country.

British Mrs. Frances Trollope, with her son and two daughters, came to New Orleans in 1827 and later went by steamboat up the Mississippi and Ohio Rivers to Cincinnati. Mrs. Trollope was writing a book about American manners and customs, so she and her children kept careful notes of everything they saw.

"On the first of January, 1828," she said, "we embarked on board the *Belvidere*, a large and handsome boat; though not the largest or handsomest of the many which displayed themselves along the wharfs. . . . We found the room destined for the use of the ladies dismal enough, as its only windows were below the stern gallery; but both this and the gentlemen's cabin were handsomely fitted up, and the latter well carpeted; but oh! that carpet! I will not, I may not describe its condition; indeed, it requires the pen of a Swift to do it justice. Let no one who wishes to receive agreeable impressions of American manners, commence his travels in a Mississippi steam-boat; for myself, it is with all sincerity I declare, that I would infinitely prefer sharing the apartment of a party of well-conditioned pigs, to the being confined in its cabin."

These are strong words, and they give us a fairly good picture of how dirty some steamboats were inside, in spite of their handsome exterior. Mrs. Trollope spoke as a housewife. That carpet! she exclaimed, and one can almost see her wishing for a good, stout broom and laying to with it, while the dust flew.

But they did have a wonderful journey and made the most of it.

"The weather was warm and bright, and we found the guard of the boat, as they called the gallery that runs round the cabins, a very agreeable station; here we all sat as long as light lasted, and sometimes, wrapped in our shawls, we enjoyed the clear bright beauty of American moonlight long after every passenger but ourselves had retired. We had a full complement of passengers on board. The deck, as is usual, was occupied by Kentucky flat-boat men, returning from New Orleans, after having disposed of the boat and cargo which they had conveyed thither, with no other labour than that of steering her, the current bringing her down at the rate of four miles an hour. We had about two hundred of these men on board; but the part of the vessel occupied by them is so distinct from the cabins, that we never saw them, except when we stopped to take in wood; and then they ran, or rather sprung and vaulted over each other's heads to the shore, whence they all assisted in carrying wood to supply the steam engine; the performance of this duty being a stipulated part of the payment of their passage."

Those early steamboats must have been rather miserable affairs, if foreign travelers were a judge. Listen to Charles Dickens, who came to America in 1842, and whose visit along the rivers is still having repercussions, especially at Cairo, Illinois, which he much maligned in his book, *American Travels*.

". . . these western vessels are . . . foreign to all the ideas we are accustomed to entertain of boats.

"In the first place, they have no mast, cordage, tackle, rigging, or other such boat-like gear; nor have they anything in their shape at all calculated to remind one of a boat's head, stern, sides, or keel. Except that they are in the water, and display a couple of paddle-boxes, they might be intended, for anything that appears to the contrary, to perform some unknown service, high and dry, upon a mountain top. There is no visible deck, even: nothing but a long, black, ugly roof, covered with burnt-out feathery sparks; above which tower two iron chimneys, and a hoarse escape valve, and a glass steerage house. Then, in order as the eye descends toward the water, are the sides, and doors, and windows of the staterooms, jumbled oddly together as though they formed a small street, built by the varying tastes of a dozen men: the whole is supported on beams and pillars resting on a dirty barge, but a few inches above the water's edge; and in the narrow space between this upper structure and the barge's deck, are the furnace fires and machinery, open at the sides to every wind that blows, and every storm of rain it drives along its path.

"Passing one of these boats at night, and seeing the great body of fire, exposed as I have just described, that rages and roars beneath the frail pile of painted wood; the machinery, not warded off or guarded in any way, but doing its work in the midst of the crowd of idlers and emigrants and children, who throng the lower deck; under the management, too, of reckless men whose acquaintance with its mysteries may have been of six-months standing; one feels directly that the wonder is, not that there should be so many fatal accidents, but that any journey should be safely made."

But journeys *were* safely made. Steamboats might be wrecked, but people filled them on every trip. Perhaps Mark Twain summed it all up when he said:

". . . the steamboats were finer than anything on shore. Compared with superior dwelling houses and first class hotels in the Valley, they were indubitably magnificent, they were 'palaces.' . . ."

Steamboats were part of America, part of us, part of our national expansion and history and our wild, reckless, wonderful growth. We might use clipper ships to sail grandly to China, and stout whalers to capture the black gold from the sea, might build noble frigates and schooners and brigs and all manner of tall-masted ships, and steamships and ocean liners, but it was our steamboats which conquered our inner wilderness—steamboats, those impossible darlings of the muddy inland rivers.

These craft were as romantic, dramatic, exciting, beautiful, wonderful, terrible, sordid, or magnificent as any vessel we ever lovingly built to traverse the waters of the world.

We put steamboats on the Yukon and on the Sacramento, on the Hudson and on the Delaware, on the Missouri and the Mississippi, the Cumberland, the Tennessee, the Allegheny, the Monongahela, on the Muskingum, the Red and the Black and the White and the St. Francis, on the Sunflower River and the Coldwater and the Hatchie and the Caloosahatchie, on the Yazoo and the Warrior. . . .

They meant paddle wheels smacking muddy water, two tall chimneys blowing black smoke, 'scape pipes spitting steam, exhausts thudding like heartbeats of the river, decks like a white layer cake with a lacework of white railings, and a special little glassed-in sky parlor for the pilot to sit in while he twirled the wheel and made the vessel do his bidding. This was what made people love steamboats, all this, and it compelled them to ride these creatures of the muddy rivers—and perish with them, if need be.

5. Big Mama

The *Big Mama* kept chickens on her roof, had an unfortunate tendency to break dishes, to upset houseboats and to wreck her own barges. The *Big Mama*, more formally known as the *Sprague*, is a steam towboat which retired from active duty in 1948, to the cheers of the people living along the rivers, and the relief of many of those who had to keep this monster vessel in running order. The *Sprague* had become a legend in her own life-time and probably will never be forgotten.

A big boat is always an imposing thing. It might not be as fast as a smaller vessel, but size is something to admire. A handsome white steamboat of great length and height and elegance was a sight for the country people to walk in for miles to behold, a treat to wait for around a bend of the river, a thrill to discover as it halted at a landing.

Size was the thing. After the War Between the States, steamboat dimensions almost got out of hand, each builder and owner vying with his rivals to produce the biggest, tallest, most gaudy craft that was ever seen on the river. The giant *Eclipse* started it even before the war—she certainly "eclipsed" all other boats, and only a few of them afterward reached the same awe-inspiring length, exceeding three hundred feet. Like dinosaurs, steamboats in their last days grew larger, fancier, and more clumsy.

As river traffic waned and the century drew to an end, many steamboats which had not fallen to pieces were put to use as towboats. Only a few passenger boats remained. The towboats pushed a vast acreage of barges containing coal or wood. They formed the link between the old Steamboat Era and today's thriving Diesel towboats. Even now, some of the old-time steamboats remain—the *Ste. Genevieve* as a train ferry, the *Goldenrod* as a showboat, the *Charles H. West* as a store boat, and the *General John Newton* at the University of Minnesota, the *John W. Snyder* at Marietta, Ohio, and the *James P. Pearson* at Winona, Minnesota, the latter three all museums. Some of the later models, however, still do heavy duty in the towing business.

In 1901, the biggest steam towboat was built expressly for that purpose. She had no quarters for passengers, just enough room for the fifty-five members of the crew needed to keep her working in top form. The *Sprague* was squat and not exactly beautiful, but she was powerful and invincible.

Built at Dubuque, Iowa, for the growing coal trade, the *Sprague* for nearly half a century was the biggest thing on the rivers, and her strength was tremendous. With 6,900 horsepower in her engines, the big towboat pushed the largest tows of coal afloat—pushed, not pulled. Tugboats along the coast pull their barges, but on the western rivers the towboats, with their squared-off bows and towing knees, are tied fast to their barges which are pushed as an immovable unit.

Sixty-two wooden barges carrying 67,000 tons of coal covered seven and one-half acres of water in front of the massive *Sprague*. It was a cargo which would have required a railroad train twelve miles long to duplicate. When she went into the petroleum trade in 1926, the *Sprague* hauled eleven million gallons of oil in one tow. No wonder the railroads did not view with pleasure the way in which river towboats hauled freight, and at cheaper rates besides.

The *Sprague*, fondly called the *Big Mama* by those who loved her, and unmentionable epithets by those who hated her, had strength which was sometimes just too great for her own good. She may have toted in triumph that great tow of coal safely from Louisville to New Orleans, but there was another coal tow of similar size, not often mentioned aloud, which the clumsy *Big Mama* totally wrecked. She simply lost control, rammed through her own barges and sank them all.

Nevertheless, the *Sprague* was amazing, and there was nothing else like her. Men were proud to work on the same river with her, while to be part of her crew was something to boast about, especially after her retirement, when all her cantankerousness and aggravations were forgotten. She needed twenty-five officers and thirty crew members to keep her going. She was 318 feet long, and her stern wheel, forty feet wide and forty feet long until it was cut down two feet both ways, weighed 360,000 pounds, or 180 tons.

The size and legends of the *Big Mama*, however, seemed to have grown in the telling, especially after she went to Vicksburg and retired, and rivermen got to reminiscing and improving on the stories about her. Some said that her wheel was so big that it was in the water one day and out the other; that the wheel-wash was felt all the way down to Brazil; that there were always five peg-leg crewmen aboard, just to punch holes in the cook's doughnuts, and a pile driver was used to mash the potatoes for dinner.

It was also said soberly that the framework of poles and wires on the roof was used to hold a canvas to scrape the clouds and obtain fresh water for the boilers; it didn't have to be filtered and strained to get the mud out. It was said that, if you carried eggs from the stern to the bow you'd have fryers before you got there.

But maybe this chicken story actually had its origin in the fact that Captain Eugene Hampton really did keep chickens aboard the *Sprague*.

Gene Hampton piloted the old *Sprague* during the last quarter-century of her activity. Much later, as one of the pilots on the *Delta Queen*, his stories of the *Big Mama* may have grown in the retelling. River stories, for that reason, are wonderful to listen to!

Captain Hampton said he liked fresh eggs and got tired of the kind that were sent out from shore with the boat's stores. There was plenty of room up on the roof of the *Sprague*, downright wasted space. You could have grown a field of corn up there, if there had been just a little more dirt. Instead, he installed a chicken coop, some hens and a rooster.

The Standard Oil Company was operating the *Sprague* at the time, so Captain Hampton named his rooster Soco in its honor. Soco was a friendly fowl. He had the run of the roof and liked to come up and visit in the pilothouse every morning for a bite of breakfast. He was very mannerly and never stayed long, got his visit over with, pecked tentatively at Captain Hampton's shoelace, to make sure it really wasn't edible, then went out foraging for insects on the roof. When the willow bugs were swarming in summer, killing themselves by millions against the arc lights, to lie in heaps on deck and roof, Soco came out of the pen first thing in the morning and ate his fill of this rich provender. Then he paraded back, the morning sunshine glinting on his scarlet comb and wattles, to call his hens to come and get the leavings; but not until he himself had quite finished.

"I kept old Soco for eight years on that boat," recalled Captain Hampton one day on the *Delta Queen*. "Got attached to him, too, and I felt bad when he got sick. He just squatted there in the pen and wouldn't come out, even when the willow bugs were thick. I knew he was a goner; he never let them pass before. And poor old Soco died that very day. I wrapped him in a piece of canvas and we had a burial ceremony for him. A deckhand with a nice speaking voice read the service, and we slid the body off a board into the Mississippi, like a funeral at sea. Missed him, too. I always looked forward to his visits up in the pilothouse every morning."

Captain Hampton got another rooster, a big Brahma red with spurs four inches long, but he was a poor substitute for Soco. The new cock stood three feet high and had a temper that would have faced up to a bull. He wouldn't let anyone come near him or the hens, and when Captain Hampton tried to gather the eggs, the Brahma tried to knock him down and rip him with the vicious spurs.

So the rooster was finally served for dinner, but was so tough that no one could manage to eat a bite. The remains went with scant ceremony into the river.

Shore dwellers were thankful when the *Sprague* was finally retired in 1948. She may have been big and fine to look at, her enormous red and gray wheel accenting her coal-smudged whiteness, but her wheel wash was so strong that it sucked water out from shore and then sent it back in a small tidal wave. It knocked out fishing boats, swamped motorboats, even wrecked fishing camps, while owners of houseboats had a particular hatred for the *Sprague*.

One day as the *Sprague* came down the Mississippi to Caruthersville, Missouri, the captain had noticed that houseboats along shore were rocking and beating about in the wheel wash. By the time the *Sprague* had tied up to the landing, two women came storming down the bank and on board, demanding to see the captain. The *Big Mama* was in trouble again! After a trip, the company was always getting letters from people along shore, saying the *Sprague* had ruined something and wanting damages.

"Where's the captain of this boat?" one of the women screeched. "That-there big tub come along and her wash mighty nigh swamped us! Rocked our houseboat till all my dishes done fell out'n the cupboard, and the glassware crashed off'n my shelves, and we ain't got a whole dish nor teacup nor drinkin' glass left! I demand to see the captain!"

Captain Hampton had taken off his cap, so the visitors couldn't tell who he was, and he didn't identify himself, just said that he'd seen the captain footing it up the hill to town and didn't know when he'd be back, or even what his name was. Then he suggested tactfully that, if they put down in writing what had been broken, he was sure the company would pay. The two women grumbled, but they left, and Captain Hampton drew a deep breath of relief.

"Yes, a lot of people were glad when that boat was decommissioned," he said. "I was on her when it happened. We took her to Vicksburg, up into the Yazoo Canal in front of the city, and that was the end. They've made her into a River Hall of Fame, a sort of museum, and a showboat."

Since that time, a company of Vicksburg actors has presented an old-fashioned melodrama called *Gold in the Hills*, in the *Sprague's* showboat theater. They followed the boat to Pittsburgh when she was towed upriver in 1959, to take part in the Pittsburgh Bicentennial. Just before the big boat set out on the trip, the last performance at Vicksburg was given, and, while it was going on, a storm came up. There was a good deal of wind, and, one by one, the mooring lines snapped, until only one was left. The *Sprague* began to rotate into the Yazoo.

While *Gold in the Hills* reached its dramatic climax, a greater drama was taking place in the wind and storm as the one remaining line stretched taut and the *Sprague* tugged to get free. If that rope had broken, she would have been swept down into the Mississippi, cast and audience still aboard, to an uncertain fate.

But someone suddenly discovered what had happened, hollered for help, and the boat was cautiously pulled in and tied again. When the show was over, the audience calmly filed off the landing, unaware of what had happened. The *Big Mama* had lost her chance to escape to freedom on the river.

Next day, she headed for the Mississippi, but not under her own power. It was too late for that. Her engines had been dismantled, her big wheel was dead in the water. She was tied to the side of a Diesel towboat, the *Western*, after a Vicksburg send-off which included Southern belles in hoop skirts and, of all things, a bevy of cancan dancers in ruffled petticoats. A tow of barges was fastened in front of the *Big Mama*, just as if she were working again, not being towed like another barge. A helpless museum piece, the *Sprague* was conducted up the Mississippi to the Ohio, where the *Lehigh* took over from the *Western*, to haul the *Sprague* the rest of the way to Pittsburgh. On the little *Lehigh*, Captain Emory Tucker was not at ease. He was totally thankful when, at last, his bulky cargo was delivered.

"She was straining to the starboard all the way up," he commented wearily. "I know it's been an honor to bring the *Big Mama* up the river—but by golly, somebody else can take her back! I don't see how pilots stood it all those years when they had to baby the old girl along!"

Yet the *Lehigh* managed, in spite of this ever-threatening

difficulty. At night, she signaled towns and passing boats not only by means of her whistle and radio-telephone, but by crossing searchlights in a big white X. This was the old monogram of the *Sprague*—scissors of light which were the big vessel's way of saying:

"Lay over. *Big Mama's* coming round the bend!"

The biggest steam towboat was met at Pittsburgh by the smallest stern-wheel steamboat. Built by Captain Frederick Way, Jr., of Sewickley, Pennsylvania, the little *Lady Grace* came down to greet the huge, inanimate guest—extremes in size meeting in the river!

The *Lady Grace* was a homemade boat. She was thirty feet long and ten feet wide, with twin chimneys crowned with cast-iron feathers. The stern-wheel of the *Lady Grace* turned over briskly, and her pilothouse and cabin were big enough for half a dozen people. The little vessel was like a floating museum. In her construction were parts of many other vessels and things. The pilotwheel was made from the top of an old oak school desk. The wire railing came from the steam packet *Queen City*, which was dismantled in 1933, after serving on the rivers since 1887. The brass roof bell had been on the towboat *La Belle*. The brass foot-brake pedal once was part of the towboat *Crescent,* and there were fragments of the steamer *Delta Queen,* obtained when she was being remodeled at Dravo Shipyard.

Many people had a hand in constructing machinery, paddle wheel, hull and jigsaw decoration of this choice little confection of a steamboat. Whereas many of the old-time big white steamers were likened to a birthday cake in elegance and snowy beauty, the *Lady Grace* was a very special little French pastry of a vessel.

On the day the *Sprague* was opened to the public, there were elaborate ceremonies, including a steamboat breakfast aboard the old boat. Later, the little *Lady Grace* paddled out into the Allegheny River, not far from the enormous *Sprague*, to where the current down from the hills was rapid as it went to join the Ohio at the Golden Triangle.

There a wreath of flowers was laid upon the river in honor of all past and present rivermen and, more subtly, honoring all the steamboats, past and present, which were the reason for those thousands of rivermen being there at all. As the flowers touched the eager water, a cannon salute was fired from another boat, and the wreath moved slowly and dramatically away on the current, heading downstream on waters many a steamboat before the old *Sprague* used to know.

6. The Wreck of the Golden Eagle

Many a boy and many a man watching the Mississippi flowing past a riverbank town have longed to be traveling on that stream. From river towns have come most of the crews for steamboats and other craft. The river was in their blood, and there was no more logical or suitable place for such a boy or man to work than on one of the boats he so admired. Most steamboat builders and owners were from such places, too. The compelling lure of the Mississippi infected boy and man, and all the handsome steamboats down through the years were their dreams, their handiwork and their possessions— that is, their possessions up to a certain point.

Up to a certain point, for a man can no more wholly own a steamboat than he can own a slice of the river. He can only sink his money and his work and his lifetime into the building and managing and operation of steamboats; he can see

55

them come and go, as he himself can see his years come and go. And the rivermen—the steamboat owner, the pilot, and the mate and the deckhand and the engineer, when they die, most often are buried in a cemetery on a bluff above the river, where its glimmer can make sun-shadows on a granite headstone, and river winds may forever sweep across the grass.

A good many steamboat companies did not begin and end with one man. Many companies became dynasties. The founder of the line handed it on to his sons or to his brother's sons, and they in turn to their children, even though an era itself might have been fading and a dynasty ending. When that happened, the last boat became a sentimental thing to cherish, as if it were almost endowed with immortality.

Such a line was the Eagle Packet Company of St. Louis, and the last of its boats, the *Golden Eagle,* lives vividly in many memories today.

The story of this boat really began with the Eagle Packet Company, in 1861, although it was not known by that name then, nor was the *Golden Eagle* even dreamed of. Two young fellows named Henry and William Leyhe, who lived with their parents beside the Mississippi, decided to build a steamboat. The young men had come from Germany as boys of six and eight, had lived for a while in St. Louis, until the terrible cholera epidemic sent them and their parents upriver, in search of a safer place in which to live. The elder Leyhe went into the lumber business at Warsaw, Illinois.

There the boys grew up, looking wistfully at the Mississippi flowing past the town and wishing, as boys will, that they were pilots on some big steamer, able to command a crew and ring bells to make the engineer obey, and to survey the river from the eminence of the pilothouse.

When they should have been helping at the sawmill, Henry and Bill were down on the river shore, skipping flat stones across the muddy water, cracking geodes to find the crystals inside, lying on their backs, counting mud-dauber wasps on the cliff, and putting themselves mentally on every steamboat that paddled past. When the wheel-wash kicked up a small wave that broke at their very feet, they felt they were actually in contact with the steamboat itself, that wonderful, unattainable creature which was forever going past and leaving them behind to count mud-daubers and crack rocks.

They must have talked steamboat for years, and then, in 1861, the notion to build one was given a shove by someone else. The owner of a wrecked boat which lay across the river from Warsaw decided that that vessel was of no use to anyone in its present condition, but that the machinery, boilers and certain other items of a nonperishable nature could be salvaged, if there was anything to put them on. So the proposition was this: the Leyhe brothers should build the steamboat. The two had access to the right kind of lumber coming in to their father's sawmill. Hardware and machinery from the sunken vessel could be cleaned and put in running condition, and the owner of the latter would reap half the profits, if any.

At the sawmill, William watched the logs coming in. He laid back some of the best and straightest. Henry flagged down two men in a small boat who were coming downstream towing four long, squared-off white pine timbers from the forests of Wisconsin. The logs were fourteen by fourteen inches, and forty-four feet long. Sticks of wood came large in those days.

The Leyhe brothers scraped together enough cash to buy the pine, although it cost them almost everything they had saved, which wasn't much. In fact, their funds had reached bedrock when the boat at last was finished, and they still needed a tiller line and could not buy one. So, the story goes, they cajoled their amiable mother into letting them have one of the ropes from a corded bedstead, and that did it. The

Young Eagle was finished, the salvaged machinery put in good condition, and the sternwheel began turning over with a noble splashing.

The little steamboat, which was only eighty-four feet long and fourteen feet wide in the beam, ran between Warsaw and Keokuk, about five miles. She was a reliable, regular craft which people could count on, and she immediately began to make some money for her youthful owners.

Now the Leyhe boys were convinced of what they wanted to make of their lives. They were in the steamboat business for good. As the years passed, they built other boats. The *Grey Eagle* was their second. She was a larger, finer craft than the first, but when she set off on her first trip from Quincy, Illinois, to Canton, Missouri, no passengers had appeared by departure time. There was no freight but a single crate of eggs sent by a stout farm woman to her brother's store in Canton.

The sidewheel *Grey Eagle* nevertheless sturdily made her run with the eggs riding in solitary luxury. With the twenty-five cents freight fare, the hungry captain (Henry) and the equally famished engineer (William) invested their day's earnings at the grocery store, buying enough cheese and crackers for their lunch.

The *Grey Eagle* did well after that, however, and so did the later Leyhe boats of the newly formed Eagle Packet Company. It moved to St. Louis, which was a center of trade on the middle Mississippi and a direct connection with other great ports along the rivers. Through the years there were many fine boats bearing the Eagle Packet name—the *Spread Eagle*, the *Bald Eagle*, the *D. H. Pike*, several other *Grey Eagles* and *Spread Eagles* and *Bald Eagles*, the *New Idlewild*, *War Eagle*, *Piasa*, *Alton*, the *Peoria*, the *Cape Girardeau* and others.

For years, the Eagle Packet Company operated out of St.

Louis, until finally the two old men who had been the youths who had founded the line turned the active work over to their sons. The Eagle Boat Store was begun in St. Louis, to service steamboat and towboat needs. It became known up and down the rivers as the place where boatmen could find what they needed—lines, lanterns, lubricating oil, no matter what.

Every now and again, trouble struck the Eagle boats, as trouble has always plagued river craft. There were sinkings and fires and destruction by ice. The latter was a great menace on the Upper Mississippi and the Illinois as well as on the Ohio. Rivermen always hoped that some year there might be year-round trade as far as the St. Louis area, but every winter the ice moved down out of the north, jamming the river. Even if the Mississippi did not always freeze solid, floating ice obstructed paddle wheels, water froze on the bucket planks and otherwise halted service. The Eagle Packet Company usually sent its boats to winter in a warmer place, down in the mouth of the Tennessee River, just off the Ohio at Paducah.

Then came the terrible winter of 1917–18. The bitter breath of deep cold and a tightening of ice moved along the rivers. The *Spread Eagle*, the *Grey Eagle*, the *Alton* and the *Peoria* were taken down to winter quarters on the Tennessee. The *Bald Eagle* was safely up in the shipyard at Paducah for repairs, and the *Piasa* was still at St. Louis.

That was a time when the Mississippi froze solid from its source to a point far south of the mouth of the Ohio. The Ohio itself was a jumble of immobilized icebergs and floes frozen in a mass, while even the Cumberland, the Kentucky and the Tennessee froze. The Eagle boats were stuck in the ice and so were many others. And when the breakup came a few weeks later, and the Ohio began to rumble and thunder and rip apart, surging downstream, the Tennessee, the Cum-

berland and the Kentucky did likewise. A great runoff up
in the hills raised the water level, and the ice mass broke and
surged and ground and pounded with a great tumult as it went
down to join the awe-inspiring Ohio. And the Eagle boats,
four of them, were literally ground to bits, broken like thin
boxwood, crushed, mashed, splintered, destroyed. People on
shore could only stand by and watch with horror, and no
one could do anything to save a single boat of the dozens that
were smashed that winter by the big ice.

It was this disaster, leaving the Eagle Packet Company with
only two vessels, that prompted the decision, in the spring of
1918, to buy an additional boat, an old southern cotton
steamer. She was remodeled and renamed the *Golden Eagle*.
And this, of all the Eagle boats, became the best known and
longest recalled, with a kind of undying fame which will
keep her memory alive on the inland rivers. The *Golden Eagle*
was certainly not the best of the Eagle boats, nor had she
the size and elegance of such massive vessels as the *Grand
Turk*, the *Great Republic* or the *J. M. White*, nor did she
have the speed of the *Robert E. Lee*. But the *Golden Eagle*
had character. She had personality and, later, a certain immortality.

A few years after securing the *Golden Eagle*, the company
built its first steel-hull vessel, the third *Cape Girardeau*, also
destined for fame. There were elaborate christening ceremonies, honoring not only the boat but also Captain Buck
Leyhe, son of one of the founders and beloved up and down
the rivers. He operated the *Cape Girardeau* as a popular tourist
steamer on the Illinois and Mississippi, on the Tennessee and
the Ohio.

But as the years were piling up on Captain Leyhe, so were
the years bringing changes to the rivers themselves. River
boats were on the wane. One by one, they were being sold

or dismantled, or else being left where they lay wrecked in the river. Trains and buses and motor cars were luring the traffic away. Some people still liked to take excursions on the rivers, but they were not abundant enough to make it a paying proposition for a company to run expensive boats and reimburse their crews and officers. Many companies sold out.

The Eagle Packet Company hated to dispose of a business that had lasted almost a century. Even though the boat store was still doing well down on the St. Louis waterfront, it was unthinkable for Captain Buck to give up steamboats altogether. So the decision was made to sell one, either the all-wood *Golden Eagle* or the steel-hull *Cape Girardeau*, and try to make a go with the remaining vessel.

By that time, there weren't very many buyers around for steamboats of any kind. The hardy Greene Line, over at Cincinnati, was still flourishing, however. The owners were interested in acquiring another boat, but their insurance policy would not permit them to operate anything but a steel-hull vessel. So the Greenes bought the fine, big *Cape Girardeau* and renamed her the *Gordon C. Greene*, in memory of the head of the family, Captain Gordon C. Greene.

That left the *Golden Eagle* based on the Mississippi. Suddenly there arose a feeling of affection for this surviving member of a long and honorable line. People who had ridden the boat banded together to form the Golden Eagle Club, later known as the Golden Eagle River Museum Foundation.

By 1939, the *Golden Eagle* was still popular, although she had certainly left the Steamboat Era behind her and was really only a relic of the past. It was in that year that she was challenged to a race by another boat more than two thousand miles away—the *Delta Queen*, over on the Sacramento River in California. She and the *Eagle*, on April 22, 1939, were to run an equal distance on their respective rivers, to see which was faster.

It was an exciting race—what steamboat race was not?—
well publicized in the newspapers and on the radio. It was a
sudden cast-back to the past, with modern embellishments.
People who had been unaware that there were any steamboats left, much less some with spunk enough to drum up a
race, followed the news of the event with interest.

And the *Golden Eagle* won the race. Her triumph, however, did not last very long. In June, 1941, when the Mississippi
was flooding, her pilot lost his bearings and rammed into a
submerged dike near Chester, Illinois, below St. Louis. A
great hole was torn in the wood hull, but the gallant steamboat managed to get to the rocky, flooded shore, where all
the passengers escaped to safety. Such had not always been
the case in wrecks of the past. This part of the river, the old
Graveyard Stretch, usually took a dreadful toll of human
lives when a steamboat was wrecked. The passengers of the
Golden Eagle stood on the bank and unhappily watched the
boat sag into the muddy flood.

Days later, the water dropped. When Captain Leyhe came
to gaze on his steamboat's dismal remains, he found, to his
delight, that the *Golden Eagle* was now actually resting on
the shore itself and could be salvaged and refloated. Work was
hastened so it would be accomplished before another rise in
the river further damaged the boat. To everyone's surprise
and pleasure, the old craft was released, cleaned up and repaired, the mud scraped out of her cabins and pilothouse, the
engines fixed up, and she was relaunched, as good as ever.
The *Golden Eagle* was traveling the river again!

Then came World War II. The *Golden Eagle* now needed
a new boiler, but boilers for steamboats were not attainable
in those days of tight priorities, so the vessel was sold. The
last boat of the Eagle Packet Company went into other hands.
Not until 1946 did she run again.

This was a year of brief and poignant glory for the old

steamboat that celebrated the century which had passed since the founders of the Eagle Packet Company came to America. There was another furious race between two steamboats which were racing again just for the fun of it, to prove that steamboat contests still existed—the *Gordon C. Greene* challenging her former sister ship, the *Golden Eagle!*

Smokestacks streaming black smoke, whistles blowing, people shouting and cheering from banks and bridges, the two boats came up the river at a fast clip, almost neck and neck, like a *Currier and Ives* print. But this time the *Golden Eagle* lost.

Soon afterward, the new owners sold her to the St. Louis Shipbuilding and Steel Company, where she was carefully repaired and redecorated as a beautiful example of an old steamboat with many years of usefulness still remaining. By now, she was a fixture on the rivers. Affection for her extended for many miles along the waterways.

On May 16, 1947, a shining white *Golden Eagle* backed out of the shipyard and paddled up to the landing to take on passengers. Then, with a tooting of whistles and a ringing of bells, with steam gauges up and paddle wheel revolving, she circled in the Mississippi and said good-by to St. Louis for the last time. She headed grandly downstream in the spring sunshine, bound for the Tennessee River. This was the initial trip of what was expected to be a very good season. She had almost a hundred passengers aboard, including stout old Captain Buck Leyhe, who went along for the ride.

Captain Buck, smoking his usual big cigar and ensconced on a big chair because he had trouble with his legs those days, could find nothing to criticize with the way in which his former boat was being operated. He got himself up the stairs to the pilothouse to sit and reminisce with the pilot for a while; it was like old times again.

But after midnight, when all the passengers were asleep,

mists rose over the river. The pilot suddenly was unsure of his exact whereabouts; then his rudders jammed. With a sickening crunch, the *Golden Eagle,* out of control, ran hard on Grand Tower towhead, seventy-eight miles above Cairo. Most of the passengers, however, slept serenely on, unaware that anything had happened.

At first it was believed that no real damage was done, but when the engineer hurried upstairs, pale to the eyebrows, to report that water was coming in fast and was already flooding the furnaces, everyone in the crew knew that it was the end. The passengers were hastily wakened and told to dress and pack as quickly as possible. Although the boat was still largely above water, she was listing badly, and her hull was filling.

In the position in which she lay, the old wooden structure was twisted and warped, breaking up fast—the certain fate of this type of vessel, once it started to rip. In the glare of the searchlights, the passengers, in a daze, got to shore, scarcely yet believing the full extent of the tragedy. They had all read about steamboat wrecks, but those were events in the past; they were part of the dangerous Steamboat Era of a hundred years ago. It seemed preposterous that such a thing should be happening to them, today.

In the darkness, they stood or sat on the muddy, lonely, shadowy, willow-grown island on which the boat had rammed herself. They all gathered around Captain Leyhe, who sat unhappily on a chair, a blanket over his knees and his cigar gone out. The chair legs, under his weight, slowly settled into the mud. By dawn, the poor captain was sitting with his feet almost straight out and the chair sunken to the seat in the pliable mud. And still he sat, chewing his cold cigar, watching the *Golden Eagle* die.

The passengers watched in fascination and awe as the lights of the boat went out. When the generators were flooded, it was as if a black hand swept across the lights and extinguished them forever. Only flashlights were left now to illuminate the slowly paling night blackness.

There was a sudden, spine-tingling sound of breakage in the tilting boat as dishes and glassware slid off shelves and crashed to bits. Windows broke in a cascade of splintering glass and brittle noise. There was a diminishing hissing of steam as the water rose in the engine room and the fires went out—and then silence. There was only an occasional sigh now as the wood in the old hull pulled gently apart.

As dawn came, birds were full of unconcerned song in the willows, the mists rose from the river, and May sunshine spread placidly across the waters, as if nothing whatever had happened in the night. The *Golden Eagle* looked even worse by daylight. Her structure was contorted in an agonizing position. Terribly broken, it had sunk halfway down in the muddy river . . . finished.

A passing towboat, the *Linda Chotin*, discovered the wreck and the refugees on the island and took them off, gave them breakfast and a ride back to St. Louis. But poor Captain Buck Leyhe could only remember the ruin of his favorite boat and, for a long time, he would not be consoled.

It was the end of an era, the end of the Eagle boats, the end of the *Golden Eagle*. Captain Leyhe lived for nine years longer, but he could never forget that night nor that perishing boat.

In St. Louis, Miss Ruth Ferris, who loves the Mississippi and its boats, and who became curator of the river room at Jefferson Memorial, was at that time assistant principal and teacher of the fifth grade at Community School. For years she had instilled some of her infectious enthusiasm for the river into every class she taught. When she learned of the wreck of the *Golden Eagle*, she could not let it be lost forever.

She determined to rescue at least the pilothouse of the old

craft and bring it to the campus of Community School as a steamboat memorial. And that is what she did.

One day, an impressive ceremony was held to dedicate the transported pilothouse to a new way of life on land— a life which would serve to teach young people the story of the rivers and about the men who navigated boats like the *Golden Eagle* ever since the first steamboat battled the Mississippi and the earthquake of 1811. The captive pilothouse might seem lonely, far from the reflective shadows and glitter of river water, but it now had a new purpose in life.

Not only would it tell of the past but it would point as well to the present active river era and to the endless future of navigation on the Ohio, the Missouri, the Mississippi, and dozens of other inland waterways. For the landscape may change, the forests may be cut down, cities replace wilderness, and Diesel engines replace steam, but the rivers and their traditions continue forever.

7. *A Dream of Steamboat Glory*

Long before the death of the *Golden Eagle*, the rivers had reached their lowest ebb in traffic and in the numbers of boats in active service. Steamboat travel in America was believed to be almost at an end. Yet in the 'twenties the first Diesel towboats were venturing on the streams, heralding the beginning of a new river era, though no one realized it then. The Steel Barge Era would populate the waterways with thousands of steel craft powered by Diesel engines, would bring business back to the waters. But the 'twenties seemed like the end, the final period to the story of river travel. In the dry summer of 1925, the slow waters of the Mississippi murmured a dirge that was felt in the towns along its shores, towns which had once been busy and prosperous and now were fading away.

At this funereal moment, the California Transportation

Company in San Francisco boldly decided to build two special steamboats—not salt-water ships, but river steamers. The company gambled on arousing the latent love of the romance of the rivers which anyone who had read Mark Twain was almost sure to have. They would put a big red paddle wheel on a white boat, give her a mellow whistle that could be heard three miles away, let her blow black smoke against the sky—and everyone would flock to admire and get aboard to ride. Mark Twain himself, who was the one most responsible for implanting this quality in Americans, would have been delighted with the story of these two new boats, the *Delta Queen* and the *Delta King*.

Plans went ahead for the construction of two super-deluxe packets which were to be finer than any known before in America, more modern, comfortable and safe. They would cost close to a million dollars each, almost three times as much as the *Great Republic* or the *J. M. White*, two of the finest, most elaborate and most costly craft of the Steamboat Era. The two new vessels would run on the San Joachin and Sacramento Rivers.

To secure expert workmanship in an almost forgotten art of steamboat building, specifications for the hulls were sent to Glasgow, Scotland, to the shipworks on the River Clyde. The two steamboats, alike as two peas, must have only the best of materials and workmanship.

The finest steel in England was produced in the mills at Birmingham and was shipped to Glasgow, where the parts were built and assembled. Slowly, with great care, the Scottish workmen constructed a pair of steamboats for the rivers of America. In Denny's Machine Shop at Dumbarton, Scotland, the machinery was built.

The workmen must have talked as they labored. They had never put together an order like this one, and the romance of their job grew as the great hulls grew. The men may have wondered about the rivers on which these fine craft would travel. They had been told that the pair would go all the way to California, to sail the Sacramento and that other river with the Spanish name, the San Joachin. But most of the men had never heard of these rivers before.

So, as the noise of the shipyard was beaten into the rivets of the *Delta Queen* and the *Delta King*, and the voices of the gulls cruising up and down the Clyde became part of the hulls, the characters of the interested Scottish workmen, too, became welded into the two boats, taking form in steel and structural outline.

The best foundries must be employed to forge A-1 quality crankshafts and wheelshafts: these came next. And there were none better than the Krupp works in Germany.

Krupp was famous for its workmanship on the great vessels of the German navy, and for the terrible guns it had produced, especially those which only a few years before had been silenced in the Armistice of 1918. No one would forget Krupp's Big Bertha pounding France from miles away. But Krupp was now a peacetime foundry, and here were forged the crankshafts and wheelshafts for two American river boats.

Near another river, then, the Rhine, one of many which would become part of the history of the *Delta King* and the *Delta Queen*, the great shafts were forged, a double order of precision-made, tremendously strong steel to turn the paddle wheels. The shafts were shipped by freighter, through the North Sea and around to Scotland, and were unloaded at the shipyard on the Clyde, where they were assembled in the finished hulls.

When the 250-foot hulls lay finished on the ways, the parts were all carefully marked; then the bolts were unbolted. The hulls were taken apart, piece by piece; they were arranged in big, compact heaps on the wharf. Cranes loaded them into the hold of another freighter. Two knocked-down river boats were about to ride inside a ship, bound for America. It was believed that nothing like this had ever happened before, and might never happen again—but, incredibly, it was happening now!

As the workmen at the Glasgow shipyard watched the loading of the dismantled hulls, they must have wondered anew about their destination and perhaps some of the men wistfully wished that they, too, were going to America, where they might one day see those twin steamboats riding on the romantic western rivers of the land of promise.

The gulls circled the oily waters of the shipyard, and the freighter's whistle blasted, echoing against the smoky buildings on shore, so that the gulls swirled up, cackling, in a sudden flurry. The ship, accompanied by diligent tugs, moved slowly down the Clyde and finally out to meet the sea. There the tugs said farewell, and the gulls followed a little way farther, in case the cook threw out some scraps from the galley, then went winging back up the river. The vessel carrying two steamboats headed out into the Atlantic, bound for a distant port on another ocean.

In an earlier day, the freighter would have had to travel down the South American coast and around through the desperate icy seas of Cape Horn, where the albatrosses coasted in the wind, then sailing up into the Humboldt Current of the Pacific, slowly fighting ice and storm and doldrum, following the same route taken by Magellan and Drake and the windjammers.

But the freighter carrying the steamboats crossed the Caribbean, passed through the locks of the Panama Canal and came out into the Pacific, having cut off thousands of miles of travel and danger. Then she headed up the coast of Mexico, north to California.

At San Francisco, the strange cargo was unloaded on barges which were towed by tugs up the Sacramento River to the shipyard at Stockton.

As if they were great jigsaw puzzles, the *Delta King* and the *Delta Queen*, under the direction of a master shipbuilder, James Burns, were put back together again. Finally when the two great steel hulls lay as finished as they had been in Scotland, their superstructures began to rise.

They were four decks high, made of American oak and pine, of mahogany from South America, with teakwood railings from Siam, and Oregon cedar from up the West Coast. The floor of the lower deck was made of yellow-brown Siamese ironbark. The staterooms were finished in mahogany and walnut. There were large plate glass windows and fine mirrors and comfortable furniture in the lounges. The salon had a fine staircase, with exquisite bronze railings. The whole staircase of the *Delta Queen* had to be hung three times before the lovely curve was considered right. There were tapestries and handsome draperies, central heating and air-conditioning.

Through the materials used in them, the two boats had become more and more international in flavor. They were composed of many kinds of woods and materials, were built by many kinds of men. And the California gulls wheeled and screamed over the shipyard as the gulls had wheeled and screamed over the shipyard on the River Clyde, and over the Rhine, and as the terns had cackled when the freighter passed through the locks of the Panama Canal.

Many voices, many men, many materials and many waters were becoming part of the intricately woven pattern in the story of these two steamboats. Even before they were finished and afloat, people were talking about them with a kind of awe, as if even the plans of the builders were becoming something they had never quite envisioned, as if some deeper creation were taking place before their eyes.

There was only one thing which did not please old-time

steamboat men: the chimney. There was only one, and who ever wanted to see a steamboat with a single chimney? The Greene Line had owned one years before, the *Greenland*, nicknamed *"One-Armed John,"* but, remembering the dramatically beautiful pictures of the *Robert E. Lee* and the *Natchez*, the *Kate Adams* and the *Queen City*, and thousands more which had conformed to the symmetry and balance of two tall, fine smokestacks, it did seem odd to see only one. Compared with those old boats, which had had a pair of forty-foot chimneys crowned with recurved feathers or petals and with a pair of triumphant deer-antlers hung between them, the two California boats, each with a single, stubby, broad chimney, seemed curiously unfinished and incomplete.

But the builders held to their plans. They were not trying to create steamboats that looked like those in the 1870's, but steamboats for today. That was why the designs were simple and distinctive, and without quantities of the gimcrack woodwork which had been part of the gaudy old boats. Instead, these two would have safety, cleanliness and the beauty of streamlined railings and posts. And one big, fat smokestack, divided into two inside. One was enough! It sat aft of the pilothouse, which was perched forward on the roof of the sundeck. And that was that.

After a triumphant launching of the twin boats in 1926, the *King* and the *Queen* made regular trips up and down the California rivers for more than ten years. They were often ridden by people going on vacations in the mountains because the river could carry them at night through the hot Sacramento Valley and land them at the state capital, close to the cool Sierras, by sunrise. Politicians going to the capital used the *Delta Queen*, known as the "six o'clock boat," between San Francisco and Sacramento.

Travel aboard was not expensive. One could get a double

room with twin beds and private bath for five dollars. There were lower-priced accommodations as well, while down on the bottom deck, a man traveling alone could secure a clean bunk for fifty cents.

The boats were much loved and admired. They provided river travel again—river travel with certain old-time embellishments brought up to date.

But ill fortune caught up with the California steamboats. When the Depression hit America, boat travel waned. The *Delta* boats hauled thousands of sacks of rice and other freight, but at last even this business was reduced until the two craft lay inactive, without much hope of ever traveling again.

But when they were about to be sold, an attack on an island in the Pacific Ocean directly affected those two internationally flavored vessels. Pearl Harbor was bombed. War flamed. And the Navy requisitioned the *Delta King* and the *Delta Queen* and painted them a somber, concealing and utilitarian Navy gray. It was a good, durable, camouflaging color, but it was probably the first time a real steam packet with a stern wheel ever traveled under such a shadow, or for such a reason.

The *Delta Queen* was renamed YFB-56, meaning Yard Ferry Boat Number 56. She and the similarly disguised *King* (YFB-57) were used to carry Navy men from destroyers and battleships in San Francisco Bay to shore and back. It was an odd experience for many a man, fresh from combat duty in the Pacific, to step off his oceangoing ship onto a real stern-wheel river steamboat, even if she was painted gray.

The *King* and the *Queen* were useful. They were doing their part in helping to win a war, but rivermen back along the Ohio and the Mississippi shook their heads in regret when they thought of what those two grand boats were doing, and how unlikely it was that they would ever again, in the traditional manner, turn their red paddle wheels on a river.

And then the war was over, finished, and the Pacific area quieted down. The need for Navy ferries diminished, so the two steamboats were towed to the boneyard of forgotten ships, in Suisun Bay, to wait for their next assignment.

8. A Queen for the Captain

An event which happened more than a century before the *Delta* boats existed was the real factor in determining what happened next to one of the boats, the *Delta Queen*. We must go back into history to find it, back to the War of 1812, when the British captured a sloop named the *Isabella*, and a steamboat company out on the Ohio River was born.

It was a wide leap from sea to river, from sloop to steamboat, but that was how it all began, how the Greene Line of Cincinnati began, and how the *Delta Queen* became destined for that port.

In the middle of the eighteenth century, an expert English anchor-smith named John Greene worked at his trade in the sea-coast town of Newport, Rhode Island. It was a time of heavy shipping, and John Greene, in his dual role as maker of anchors and mender of damaged ones, had much to do.

His sons, Daniel, Richard and John, Jr., were brought up in the ways of the sea. During the American Revolution, they served under their noted and heroic first cousin, General Nathanael Greene, one of the ablest generals of the war, perhaps second only to Washington.

Under the skilled command of their cousin, the Greene boys fought at the Battle of Brandywine, helping to save the American army from complete destruction. Later, with the war finally won, the Greenes were given grants of land, a grateful nation's thank-you to the men who had helped preserve it. Because money was scarce after the costly conflict, and because land stretched in unending abundance to the western horizons, it was easier to give a soldier a farm than to pay him cash. Most men were hungry for land, cheap land, free land, to get them beyond the Alleghenies and into the wonderful West.

General Nathanael Greene, because of his heroism at Eutaw Springs, received large tracts of land in Georgia and South Carolina, but his cousins had grants located far away, along the Ohio River above Marietta, Ohio. The three young men were not exactly pleased at having property so far from the seacoast; they would have preferred something closer to home. Their work and interests lay in the East and already had been too long neglected during the war. They were coastal men. Land lying a thousand miles from the sight and smell of sea water did not appeal to them. Besides, Captain Dan Greene had a sloop named the *Isabella* which ran out of Charleston, South Carolina, to the Orient and back. So the three Greene brothers stayed in the East and were content.

And the land out along the Ohio waited for them. In 1808, the trio took time away from their business to go over the mountains and down the Ohio to see about it, and while they were there they built a good stone house for their father, John, the anchor-smith. The elder Greene moved out to

Ohio and for some time used the house as a tavern, providing food, drink and lodging for river travelers.

The younger men went back to the East again, to take out the *Isabella* on another voyage, but the clipper ship trade, even then, was headed for trouble. The Embargo Act endangered vessels and commerce, and the War of 1812 clinched the matter: the beautiful *Isabella* was captured by the British.

The Greenes were ruined. There was nothing else to do but sell their holdings, pay off their creditors and then join their father out along the Ohio. They founded the town of Newport, named in nostalgic memory of their birthplace, far away on the edge of the sea.

They had left the ocean forever, but could not escape the lure of navigable waters. The Ohio flowed past their door, and on it were boats. The Greenes saved enough money to build a stern-wheel steamboat, another *Isabella*, far different from the sleek-lined ship the British had taken, but better fitted for an environment far from the sound and smell of the sea.

The years went by, and there came a time when the grandson of John Greene, Jr., named Gordon C. Greene, was growing up beside the Ohio. He was a sober youngster, with an inherited love of the river. His parents couldn't keep him away from the fascinating stream. He was always building something down on the shore—a little raft which sometimes fell to pieces under him, or a fleet of tiny sailboats made of chips with sycamore-leaf sails, or a real flatboat. When he was sixteen, young Gordon built himself a square-bowed rowboat and whittled out a pair of oars so that he could travel around on the river. As he grew older, he worked on steamboats and studied the river until, at twenty-one, he was able to get his first-class pilot's license and his master's papers.

Seven years later, two vastly important things happened

to the earnest young pilot: he had saved enough money to buy a small low-water steamer, the *H. K. Bedford,* and he married pretty Mary Becker, who loved the river, too.

Vivacious Mary set about to be a pilot. She was one of the few women to serve almost a lifetime as a licensed pilot on the Ohio. She was a zestful, attractive, outgoing young woman, known affectionately along the waterways as the Petticoat Skipper and hailed respectfully and lovingly by every passing boat.

For a long time, Captain Gordon C. Greene piloted the *H. K. Bedford* while Captain Mary Greene piloted their second boat, the *Argand.* These two and the craft which followed as the Greene Line grew were noted for having the best food on the river, the most reliable and alert crews and the cleanest cabins. They had to be. Captain Mary insisted on immaculate and comfortable living conditions wherever she was, be it boat or home. Since she rather preferred the boats to land dwellings, the former had to conform to her high standards.

In 1904, Gordon and Mary Greene bought out the White Collar Line, a rival steamboat company, and moved the Greene Line to Cincinnati, where it has been ever since, taking over the lower river trade as well as the upper.

Of the three sons born to the Greenes, one died early, but Chris and Tom grew up on the boats. Tom, in fact, was born on a bitter February day aboard the *Greenland* because the vessel was frozen in the ice of the Kanawha River, at Point Pleasant, West Virginia, and his mother couldn't get to shore for the occasion.

Both boys became pilots and masters. At their father's death, Chris Greene took over the management of the boats while handsome young Captain Tom Greene was usually in command of the *Gordon C. Greene.* Their mother was the official hostess, taking over at the controls when necessary.

She never lost that touch, that ability to pilot a big steamboat and to keep passengers happy and entertained at the same time.

It was a blow to the Greene Line when Chris Greene died suddenly in 1944, after a day of working on one of the boats during the wartime shortage of men. Captain Tom Greene and faithful "Ma" Greene herself continued operating the *Gordon C. Greene* during the remainder of the Second World War. Boat travel had suddenly become popular—priorities on trains and planes, and shortages of gasoline, had curtailed other kinds of vacation jaunts. The Greene Line was doing very well indeed. And that was when Captain Tom Greene began thinking of what he could do if he had another good boat, fireproof, steel-hull, well built. He and most of the other rivermen in the Middlewest knew all about what had been happening to the *Delta* boats out in California. Suddenly, Captain Greene decided to have one of them for himself.

It was 1946, and the war was over. Two perfectly good stern-wheelers were laid up and doing no one or themselves any good. A boat needs to be used. Inactivity is ruinous. And so, when word came that the two *Deltas* were up for sale, Captain Greene recklessly put in his bid and, probably because there were no others, he found himself the owner of the *Delta Queen*, sold for $46,500.

The *Queen* was his. He had bought himself a piece of river royalty. But neither Captain Greene, nor anyone else, at that interesting moment, had any idea as to how he would get a river boat from Suisun Bay to Cincinnati.

Here was a big, shallow-draft vessel, extending a mere seven feet into the water and standing fifty feet above it, with a big, clumsy wheel and its support thrusting out thirty-five feet to the rear. She belonged in quiet river water, not on the waves of the surging Pacific.

There were a good many jovial suggestions, such as knocking down the *Delta Queen* to her separate parts again and pack-muling them, piece by piece, over the mountains from the Columbia River to the headwaters of the Missouri, then by towboat down the Missouri to the Mississippi, and up the Ohio to Cincinnati, home base. There was also the notion of letting the *Queen* come by her own power via the Pacific Ocean and the Gulf of Mexico. But those who casually suggested this had never seen the Pacific Ocean on a brisk day!

Captain Frederick Way, Jr., noted steamboat captain and author of river books, a good friend of the Greenes, thought perhaps he could do the latter. He had navigated inland rivers; and he knew steamboats as well as or better than any man alive. Captain Greene had delegated him to go out to California and bring home the *Delta Queen*, leaving the method up to Captain Way.

They both knew that towboats had been taken across the Gulf of Mexico, all the way down to the Magdalena River in South America, and that most of them had survived the trip. They also knew what had happened to the first one which had attempted the journey under her own power. The vessel had found herself hung up on two waves in a storm. The boat broke in two and sank, and the crew had to be rescued with no little difficulty from the sea. After that, towboats were generally crated and towed to their overseas destinations. But what about steamboats? Yes, what about them?

Captain Greene and Captain Way, with the one-track minds of men in love with rivers and boats, and oblivious to the dangers of such impossible bodies of water as the oceans, were confident that a big, steel-hull steamboat of the *Queen's* stature, strength and stability, with excellent engines and hull almost as strong as that of an ocean liner, could take off from California and, hugging the shore, could make the trip under her own power. It sounded reasonable.

It did, that is, before the two men, several weeks later, had taken a long and thoughtful look at the Pacific Ocean, had listened to the melancholy and ominous calling of the fog horns out in the bay, or had seen the Pacific in a storm. It was also before they had heard about the *chubascos*, violent tempests boiling out of the Gulf of Tehuantepec, off Mexico, which are fatal to small craft.

Tom Greene trusted Fred Way's judgment. But, the former warned his friend, if he did take the *Delta Queen* to sea, and things grew too rough and dangerous, he must think only of saving himself and his crew and let the *Queen* go down to her death. This suggestion probably put Captain Way in a sober frame of mind. And the fog horns haunted him.

He went to see the Coast Guard Commander for written permission to remove the *Queen* and take her to sea.

"Where did you say you were taking that vessel?" asked the Commander suspiciously.

"Cincinnati."

"*Cincinnati?* Cincinnati, *Ohio?* And how do you propose to take that fresh-water egg beater to Cincinnati, sir?"

"Why, under her own power, most likely," began Captain Way, blinking. "Why not? She's a good boat—strong engines, steel hull. She's fit. The Navy used her out on San Francisco Bay."

"Why *not?* Sir, I will never permit such a foolhardy plan to remove any boat from this port! The only way in which you could do so would be to register this preposterous mud-puddle vessel under a foreign flag. *But under the American flag*—she stays where she is!"

"Then how can we get her to Cincinnati?"

"By crating her up, of course, and hauling that so-called ship of yours by tugboat to wherever you want to go! Good day, sir!"

Captain Way was more than a little relieved to know, now

that he had had a look at the heaving gray hugeness of the
Pacific Ocean, he would not have to personally navigate the
Delta Queen upon that massive body of water. If he had, she
might now be lying on the floor of the sea, crusted with
barnacles and with fish swimming in her staterooms.

Captain Greene came out to San Francisco, and, together
with Captain Way, he went out to Suisun Bay, to find the
Delta Queen. Until now, they had never seen her, only her
photographs, but they felt it would not be too difficult to find
a river stern-wheeler among the dead and discarded ships in
the boneyard. Here the Cincinnatians found a terrible confusion of hulks and hulls, mostly seagoing vessels, a square
mile or more of them, lined up in dismal rows. The *Queen* was
still camouflaged in her gray paint besides, so was effectively
hidden.

But they located her at last. In the thickening fog which
was rolling in from the Pacific, Captain Way and Captain
Greene went aboard for the first time.

And they knew then, even in the veiling of wet Pacific
mist that wreathed itself around the *Queen's* pilothouse and
silvered the teakwood railings and decks, that, although she
had barnacles caked on her quiet stern wheel and hull and
still bore the anonymous character of Navy gray, they had
bought a real *Queen.* She would find her place in the world
at last when she came to the Mississippi and the Ohio. A
great lady in disguise, the *Delta Queen* rocked inertly in the
swells of the rising tide.

The two went to the Maritime Commissioner's office to
get permission to remove the *Delta Queen* from Suisun Bay.
They found the Commissioner in a bad mood and not likely
to concede to any request they were apt to make.

"Speed! Speed! Always wanting to get out a ship in a hurry,
without any advance warning! I'm getting fed up with it. And

who did you say you were?" he added, glancing up at Captain Way's pleasant face and at handsome Captain Tom Greene.

"Captain Frederick Way, Jr."

"Captain of what, where?"

"Well, I was captain of the steamboat *Betsy Ann*, among others. And this is Captain Tom Greene of the Greene Lines, who's just bought the *Delta Queen*, and we want—"

"Well, well, I'm glad to see both of you!" interrupted the beaming official. He sprang from his chair to shake hands, suddenly cordial. "I'm a Mississippi River man myself, or was, and I should have known you were, too."

"What boat were you on?"

"I was engineer on the cotton stern-wheeler *Natchez*, in the New Orleans–Vicksburg run. That was a great life. Don't know why I ever left it! Now, what was it you wanted?" he added.

"The *Delta Queen?* Easy! Now, here is what you do."

And so what looked at first like a long, tedious delay was solved by a few minutes of Mississippi steamboat talk, the magic of the rivers which touches men and leaves them somehow different. Like Marquette and Jolliet, they, too, must have drunk of the Mississippi and so had it forever in their blood!

In the fog, the *Delta Queen* was detached from the ships surrounding her, taken away for the last time from the *Delta King's* company, and was hauled by tugboat up to the Fulton Shipyard at Antioch. That was the first step in the *Queen's* rejuvenation, her return to life, the first lap in her most amazing voyage. Deserted, the *Delta King* rocked soddenly on the tide.

At the shipyard, the *Delta Queen* was carefully covered with 50,000 feet of spruce planking, as if she were a big piece of furniture being crated. She was nailed up two decks high, and a big tarpaulin was tied down over the open chimney, to keep rain and salt water out of the boilers.

While all this was going on at the shipyard—after Captain Greene had gone back to the Ohio River, leaving Captain Way in charge—a tall old man, dignified and quiet, came to say goodby to the *Delta Queen.*

There was little enough of her still visible above the planking, though pilothouse and sundeck were unmistakable.

"I want to see that boat of yours before she sails," said the visitor, looking up at the *Queen's* silent bulk.

"Well, we're always glad to have visitors, Mr. . . ."

"Jim Burns. I—built the *Delta Queen.*"

There was a sudden quiet in that shipyard. Captain Way recalls how the riveters stopped their work, the noise of the motor crane, the racket of the hammers, seemed suddenly stilled, with only the sea gulls keening and mewing from where they lined up on a roof top. Men laid down their tools and walked toward the tall, spare old man.

"Sir, I'd like the honor of shaking your hand," said one of the workmen, holding out his grimy palm. "I'd like to say I shook the hand of the builder of the *Delta Queen.*"

The others lined up there in the shipyard, and each one greeted the man who had constructed the *Delta Queen* twenty years earlier. He was eighty-four now, and had come to look for the last time on the boat which he could never forget, and which had a strange hold on his life, just as she has had a hold on other lives, down through the years.

"I'd surely admire to see her on the Mississippi River," he said wistfully, drinking coffee as he sat in stateroom 215, which Fred Way had fitted up for his own during the stay in the shipyard.

"You come on down to Cincinnati, Mr. Burns, and we'll see that you have a lifetime pass to ride the *Delta Queen!*"

"No, son, it's too late. I haven't that much lifetime left. I'll never get that far now. But it would be a pure pleasure, it certainly would!"

Work went on quickly. The bow of the boat was carefully boarded up in a sharp V-shape, like a cowcatcher, to plow through the waves and prevent damage to the boat when a big one hit. The thirty-ton paddle wheel was somehow removed from its boxing and placed inside the boat, an operation which must have required no little ingenuity, strength and skill. Marine inspectors arrived and O.K.'d the job. The insurance inspectors came around. Everything was fine. Captain Way and two rivermen from the Ohio were laying in supplies, emergency rations, life rafts and other items, preparing to accompany the *Queen* on her voyage, even though there would be no navigating to do. She would merely be towed like a barge behind a tugboat.

More and more, as they heard the fog horns blowing and blatting when the daily fog rolled in, they felt less and less cheerful about the coming trip. No matter how sturdy the *Queen* was, or how well crated, she was still a flat-bottom steamboat with a seven-foot draft and no keel, and riding her was going to have its uncomfortable and perhaps dangerous moments, out on the waves of the stormy high seas.

To avoid the worst of the weather, to miss the *chubascos*, the trio knew they must go in April and May. They urged greater speed in finishing the work, for April was already upon them, and time was slipping by fast. A sturdy tug named the *Osage* was chartered to pull this crated-up steamboat, now designated a sea-going barge, and deliver her to the shipyard at New Orleans.

By the middle of April, everything was ready. People all over the country, by this time, were anxiously awaiting news of what was going to happen. Newspapers and radios had

made a big thing of this intended voyage of the *Delta Queen*
in the springtime of 1947.

And then the maritime unions stepped in and changed things
in short order. The unions complained that inexperienced
Mississippi River sailors were about to ship as crew on a
fantastic vessel which was taking to the high seas, three men
whose licenses applied only to the inland rivers. This, they
protested, was clearly illegal and not to be tolerated by the
unions protecting the interests of seamen. It was required, said
the unions firmly, to put aboard the *Delta Queen* a crew of
ten properly qualified salt-water sailors, complete with captain, mate and engineers, even though the *Queen* had no
working parts now and was merely being towed by a very
efficient tugboat with its own crew. But she was still a vessel,
they insisted, which by law must have a crew.

No amount of protest could budge the decree. The unions
had it in their power to delay things so long that the voyage
could not be made safely before bad weather set in. With the
Mexican storms breathing down their necks, Captain Way and
his rivermen from Cincinnati got off the *Delta Queen* and
unhappily watched the new crew get on.

Two of the seamen were Russian and one came from Fin-
land. The second mate was Chinese. The rest were a rough
lot generally. The captain himself was a quiet, pleasant German named Frederick Geller. And Captain Tom Greene was
going to have to pay nearly ten thousand dollars extra as
wages for this unneeded crew and send them home by air at
his expense, from New Orleans.

9. The Terrible Voyage of the Delta Queen

On the morning of April 17, when sunrise was coloring the waters of the river, the tug *Osage* attached her lines to the *Delta Queen*, tooted a whistle in farewell and moved slowly down the San Joachin, to where it joins the Sacramento.

Captain Frederick Way and his men stood on the dock and watched the *Queen* depart without them. Mists curled around her sides, and there was a depressing air of silence about the big vessel. Without her big paddle wheel beating waves in the water, without smoke issuing from her broad chimney, without a pilot at the wheel, she was not really a steamboat, only a large piece of freight, lifeless, inanimate.

No one said very much, but every man on the wharf was

wondering what would happen to the *Queen* out in the Pacific; was wondering if they would ever see her again, or if this was their last sight of the handsomest steamboat still afloat. They went back to their hotel, finally, gathered up their belongings and silently took the train back to Cincinnati to wait.

As if she rebelled against being sold, the *Delta Queen* refused to behave. She bucked and skewed about, wouldn't follow obediently after the *Osage*. Captain King discovered that he had tied her wrong. He had been trying to tow her stern first, which was an insult, no doubt, and hurt her dignity.

So he let go the stern line and maneuvered around to hook on a head line. Suddenly and momentarily free in the river, the *Delta Queen* broke away and escaped.

The wind caught her. She picked up speed, sailed briskly across the river, promptly ran herself onto a mudbank—and there she stuck, her brief freedom done. An airplane circling over to watch her departure took a picture, and soon the newspapers over the country were blaring the story that the *Delta Queen* had refused to be sent away from her home state of California.

As a curious coincidence, at about the same time, another seagoing *Queen* got into trouble. The British liner, *Queen Elizabeth*, chose to run aground on a mud flat near Southampton, England. Solidly and determinedly stuck in the mud, the pair of *Queens*, separated by thousands of miles, occupied the interest and speculation of two nations.

But the *Delta Queen* was not permitted to stay long on her mudbank. Captain King fastened his lines again and pulled. The steamboat came loose and obediently followed as, once more, they set off . . . into San Francisco Bay, under Golden Gate bridge, through the Golden Gate and out at last into the Pacific Ocean. There was a northwesterly wind blowing; the weather was fine and clear; the fog had burned off for the day; and the *Delta Queen* rolled gently on the swells. She now followed docilely after the *Osage*, which was plowing determinedly through the blue water, heading south down the coast of California.

Meanwhile, the crew of ten which had shipped to ride the *Queen* very likely soon began to wish they had never come aboard. If they had figured they would have little, if anything, to do for a month, except eat and sleep and watch the sea gulls going by, at Captain Tom Greene's expense, they soon changed their minds. For the *Delta Queen* didn't belong on the waves of the relentless Pacific Ocean, not even as a crated piece of freight. A ship with a keel is stable and most often behaves, with a certain amount of allowable rolling and pitching in rough weather. The flat bottom of a river boat is all wrong on angry water and doesn't know how to act.

Instead of cutting through the waves as the *Osage* was doing, she was following the rise and fall of each swell, riding like a chip of wood. She did an enormous amount of rocking and rolling, climbing the waves, sliding down into the troughs, coasting up again. She kept up this preposterous means of navigation for the whole trip, while the salt-water sailors inside must have been seasick for a month.

To add to their woes, the weather fouled up a few days after they set off. By the time they were passing Catalina, the island itself was almost hidden in a sweeping rainstorm. The flying fish leaped up from the bow of the *Osage* and again from the snubby bow of the *Delta Queen*, then went scooting off like silver arrows into the mist and rain. And the waves grew bigger and wilder.

They rose at the defenseless *Queen* as if the whole ocean were tipping over upon her. Yet, just as an angry gray mountain of water came towering above her, the *Queen*, at the end of her hawser, slid up at a forty-degree angle and over the crest; or the waves slid under, whichever you choose. At the

same time she was sliding up and coasting down, the *Queen* was also rolling from side to side. As soon as she was over one massive wave there was another, wicked and menacing, forever and ever, big, steely mountains of water and vast hollows between.

There was rough going for several days, but the boat weathered it. Ten days after they left San Francisco, the tug pulled into the sudden quiet behind Manzanilla Breakwater, off the Mexican coast, to take on supplies. The crew went ashore and may not have been too eager to get back on, except that the pay was so good, the work lacking, and the voyage couldn't last forever, even though there were times when it began to feel like it.

After several days in port, Captain Geller on the *Delta Queen* ordered his crew aboard. Later, as they were roughly paralleling the Mexican coast, the barometer began to drop alarmingly. The sea had an ugly look, great gray-green swells heaving under the river boat and not breaking into whitecaps, with an odd sort of choppiness coming from all angles until she hardly knew which way to roll.

Soon, the *Delta Queen* was pounding and rocking heavily along as if she were confused; she wasn't trailing the tug *Osage* as well as before. Instead, she was pitching wildly and standing almost on her beam ends, nosing down at a frightening slant, plowing up again—up, somehow. She was wallowing down into the trough and pitching at such a dangerous angle that she was all but out of control.

It was three o'clock in the morning when her crew became panicky, and the men on watch roused Captain Geller, who probably wasn't getting a great deal of sleep on a boat traveling in such obvious difficulties. The men were certain that the *Queen* was going to come apart and sink with them. But when Captain Geller got up, and he and the Chinese second mate went all over the inside of the boat and examined everything, they found that she wasn't coming apart anywhere, had sprung no leaks, the boarding outside was secure. But she was still rolling so badly that it was all they could do to walk on the tipping decks.

Captain Geller's handwriting in the log of the voyage that day was scratchy, uneven, and didn't hit the lines. The logbook, now in the Inland Rivers Library in the Cincinnati Public Library, is visual evidence of what was happening along the Mexican coast on the terrible voyage of the *Delta Queen*.

Captain Geller was still uneasy. He called to Captain King to pull in closer to shore, just to be on the safe side. Then a tremendous sea slammed against the *Delta Queen* with a crash that shook her from bow to stern and rattled the windows. It sent the captain and the Chinese mate staggering against the pilothouse stair railing, and they got downstairs— a very steep descent, even in smooth weather—somewhat bruised and bumped. They found most of the crew members by this time laid out deathly seasick in their bunks.

Another heavy sea followed another, while Captain King struggled to turn in the troughs and haul the river boat gently but firmly out of danger. Those waves were nothing to fool with on a dark night, not in a river steamboat that was bucking about like a panicky buffalo.

But eventually the worst seas subsided. The *Delta Queen* continued without mishap, though still rolling, her usual marine gait. She had been built to last, even in a sea storm. Closer to shore, the boat rode more easily. The *Queen* and her escort went on down the coast of Mexico, past Guatemala and Honduras, where the rugged mountains stood blue-green and tall, with banana plantations at their bases. And past the peaks of Nicaragua and Costa Rica, perhaps past that very "peak in Darien" where Balboa is said to have stood when he discovered the Pacific Ocean.

At last, the *Osage* and her tow entered the Panama Canal Zone, short cut between oceans. Hailed by a port authority boat, she was boarded and searched for contraband, which must have taken some time, looking into all those ninety-odd staterooms. The *Queen* was untied from the *Osage*. Another tug came alongside and escorted the river boat up to the

Miraflores Locks.

Officials came aboard and Captain Geller signed papers. The Panamanian officials and the onlookers at the locks were startled to see what was coming through. They had never beheld such a preposterous craft moving from ocean to ocean, with DELTA QUEEN OF SAN FRANCISCO lettered on her life preservers, and DELTA QUEEN OF CINCINNATI on her stern. But there were no rules against admitting a stern-wheel steamboat bound for the Mississippi River, and so she moved into the Panama Canal.

The crew took on stores. Next day, the tug conducted the *Queen* through Miraflores Locks, and then through Pedro Miguel Locks. Then she was out in the Panama Canal itself, in quiet water like a river, for a change, but with jungles and mountains along the banks. Howling monkeys and gaudy toucans set up a wild serenade of noise just before dawn, and herons, much like those she would know all along the inland rivers, got up from the shallows of Gatun Lake and flapped to a farther shore as the *Queen* went past. Flocks of green parrots with yellow and scarlet heads streamed across from bank to bank.

The *Delta Queen* was taken through the Canal and locks with as much respect and care as if she were a battleship or an ocean liner. Natives stood on the shore and watched. She moved through Gatun Locks, and then she was set free. The tug *Osage*, which had gone ahead, tied on her hawser again, and they were off through the remainder of the canal, until finally they were out in the Caribbean Sea.

Immediately, the *Delta Queen* resumed her unfortunate rolling and pitching. She had been calm in the Canal, to the boundless relief of her crew, who finally felt able to sit up and take a little nourishment, but now she celebrated her freedom on the sea by being as cantankerous as she ever was in her life, doing an immense quantity of plain and fancy pitching and rolling, though there was no storm. Most of the crew retired to their bunks again. The cook, a pasty-faced, round little man who had come aboard with a hacking cough which had grown no better, managed to stir up some dinner for those who were still able to eat, and then took to his own bunk, a sick man.

And on and on they went, those two vessels, over Yucatan Channel, the deepest waters in the Gulf of Mexico, 18,000 feet in some places. The *Delta Queen* did not falter. She wallowed and rolled in the waves, but she stayed upright. There was no land in sight now, nothing but waves coming at a river boat which looked very small in their immensity, nothing in sight but the frigate birds coasting on the updrafts and the white terns crying.

One fine, calm morning, with a southeast wind blowing and a small, sweet sea running, there was land ahead. Land! The crew must have felt like Columbus sighting a continent. Soon the *Osage* shortened her hawser and turned into the channel of the Mississippi River, up Southwest Pass, moving beside green marshes and muddy hummocks that had been deposited at the very end of the river as it thrust its way 120 miles out into the sea.

Captain Geller wrote casually and laconically in the log: "Vessel riding easily up the river."

It was no wonder! The *Queen* was on familiar waters at last, on a river, after all those thousands of miles of wild ocean salt water. No wonder she was steady. The *Delta Queen*, although she had never before been on the Mississippi, had come home—and there was a solemn significance in her arrival. She had come to keep an old river tradition alive.

At Pilottown, down near the mouth of the Mississippi, the tug stood by while special pilots came aboard the *Osage* to take her up the river. Next day, they reached New Orleans, and two tugs tied on while the *Osage*, her valiant work done, let go. The *Delta Queen* was guided through the narrow Harvey Locks, across from New Orleans, and into the Harvey Canal, then into the big Avondale Shipyard on the west bank.

It was May 19, 1947, a month after leaving San Francisco Bay, that the *Delta Queen* was untied at last, and the hydraulic lift at the shipyard hoisted her into the marine ways at Avondale. The salt-water seamen who had signed on in California dallied several days longer, to lengthen their pay span. Finally, they were thankfully paid off and put on a plane bound for San Francisco. The tug *Osage* and Captain King, however, freed of their responsibility, set off to return by the long, wet route over which they had come.

10. *The Queen Comes Home*

Tom Greene and Fred Way were probably the gladdest pair of men along the Lower Mississippi when they saw the big, ungainly, boarded-up bulk of the *Delta Queen*, looming behind the diligent little *Osage* and the accompanying tugs, coming in triumph up the river from the sea. The two captains had arrived by train at Avondale Shipyard to be on hand when "Greene's *Queen*" arrived—*if* she ever got there—and there she was, apparently none the worse for her harrowing voyage over 5,378 miles of sea water.

Up on the ways of the drydock, the *Queen* was stripped of all the sea-stained boarding, all 50,000 feet of it. She had the salt washed from her windows and upper decks, from the pilothouse windows. Captain Way and Captain Greene roamed from deck to deck, looking her over and gloating at what they had caused to be brought to the Mississippi. And, in spite of all the rough weather and the *Queen's* wild cavorting, she had, after all, been stable enough for a half-empty can of paint—left by Captain Way on a cylinder timber in the engine room—to have stayed upright and unspilled!

The engines were overhauled. The great paddle wheel was put back in place. In those days, it was covered with a big, round wooden canopy or splash guard. This boxing was removed permanently later on. The massive shafts connecting the big red and white wheel with the pistons moved tentatively, like big grasshopper legs, trying themselves out. . . . The wheel turned . . . gained speed. The *Delta Queen* was coming alive!

She was at last lowered gently to the water. Under her own power, she moved out into the Harvey Canal, got up steam and went through the locks. By the time she was in the Mississippi, she was pretty much herself again. The engines thudded and the pistons worked smoothly. She left a big, white wash of waves behind her churning stern wheel.

The *Delta Queen* was working on a river again, on the river for which she must have been originally destined. There was a singular feeling of gladness and triumph in a good many hearts, and tears in a few eyes, when she started up the Mississippi. Some said, sentimentally and a little superstitiously, that it was as if the souls of all the packet boats that ever were in the past had come back to the rivers where most of them had died. The *Queen* of the Mississippi and the Ohio had indeed come home.

When she set off up the river, Captain Way was her pilot, although there were moments when he admitted that he didn't really feel like a steamboat captain but the curator of a floating museum. The men who had gone to California with him to bring home the *Queen* were in the engine room. But the deck hands were something unique in the strange history of river steamboating.

It seems that nearly everyone had been following the progress of the *Delta Queen* in the newspapers. As she set forth on the last lap of the trip, a large number of businessmen in Cincinnati and Louisville begged Captain Greene to let them come on as deck hands. They didn't know much, if anything, about decking, but they were willing to work, were in love with the river, and were devoted to steamboats. They worked hard, too, all those expensive crewmen—bankers, lawyers, merchants and whatnot. Fred Way commented wryly that an explosion aboard would have set back the business affairs of Cincinnati for a generation!

But there was no explosion, no real trouble. The voyage went smoothly and triumphantly up the Mississippi. From the jack staff fluttered the flags of all the countries which the *Queen* had passed since she left San Francisco, making quite an array of color—the flags of Mexico, Guatemala, Salvador, Honduras, Nicaragua, Costa Rica, Panama and the United States.

Homer Waxler and Walter Horne, the pilots, blew the big, sonorous whistle which stirred up some tremendous echoes against the Natchez bluffs, against the buildings of Memphis, across the sand bars and mud flats of the Mississippi.

She was saluted all along the way by every passing towboat until the river was a procession of whistles. The pilots and Captain Way must have had tired arms, waving, but everyone loved it! There had been nothing quite like this on the Mississippi, not even the Presidential Procession of steamboats in 1907, when Theodore Roosevelt headed the parade. There had been steamboats and celebrities before, but surely not a wild, glad, crazy hullabaloo like this triumphal journey of an almost legendary boat.

At Cincinnati, on July 27, 1947, she was greeted by the Greene Line Steamers officers and by Mrs. Greene and the children. Most of Cincinnati crowded down to the big, dark wharf boat, to see the new pride and joy of the rivers. But the *Delta Queen* couldn't stay long at her home base, not just now. There was much to be done before she could start to work. She went on up to Dravo Marine Ways, at Pittsburgh, where she underwent six tedious months of extensive and expensive renovating and remodeling.

All that gray paint had to be stripped off, a job which was about equal to taking the paint off a five-story house. The finest, the most modern and probably the last of the passenger steamboats was being fixed up at the same city which had built the first one, back in 1811.

A number of structural changes were made. The smoke-stack was cut down, and the upper part was made removable at will, so that it could fit under Ohio River bridges in times of high water. The paddle wheel boxing was taken off; in sudden cold weather, before boat travel stopped for the winter, ice could form and clog the wheel, while driftwood tangled inside the boxing could be a perpetual menace. Besides, whoever had heard of a Mississippi stern-wheel steamboat with her beautiful big wheel hidden?

On the California rivers, the canopy had kept flying spray from wetting the passengers, but this was solved in the remodeling by a splash guard opposite the wheel, leaving it visible but protecting the passengers. Part of the joy of traveling on the *Delta Queen* is found in watching the big wheel at work, a thrilling sight as it digs deeply and sets up a series of powerful breakers, combing over white in the distance.

The forward decks were all made bigger, extending out in the contours of the bow, to give more promenade and sun-deck space. The lower deck, which once had carried freight and the automobiles of the passengers, was remodeled. Its wonderful golden Siamese ironbark floor was retained, sanded, polished and left bare for the new dining room, pantry and bar, while the salon on the cabin deck, formerly the dining room, was changed into a corridor with writing desks, and extra staterooms opening out on each side. The domed ceiling and tapestries were removed and the ceiling was lowered, to permit more staterooms with private baths on the texas deck. Inside and out, she was repainted, redecorated. New furniture was bought.

The *Delta Queen* was completed in the summer of 1948. She came down to Cincinnati and set off on her first cruise on the Ohio, to Cairo and back. Year by year after that, while changes came still further to the rivers, removed more steamboats and added larger, finer and more powerful steel towboats, the *Delta Queen* continued to operate and to enlarge her itinerary. She was making four annual twenty-day trips to New Orleans and back; a twenty-day autumn journey to St. Paul–Minneapolis, on the Upper Mississippi; week-long trips to Kentucky Lake via the Tennessee River; up to Chattanooga and Lookout Mountain; a ten-day trip to Reelfoot Lake, in Tennessee, and one of similar length to Pittsburgh. And sometimes there were prosperous years, sometimes they were more lean.

The lean years were upon Greene Line Steamers in 1957. Captain Tom Greene had died suddenly, one day in 1950, a few hours after being removed from the *Delta Queen* to a hospital. His mother had died the year before, in her stateroom on the *Queen*. These had been years of tragedy and trouble. The steamboats *Tom Greene* and *Chris Greene* had been sold and turned into barges. The *Gordon C. Greene* had been sold, but still there were not enough people who seemed interested in filling all the trips on the one remaining Greene Line vessel, the *Delta Queen*.

And then, at last, there came a grim day in January, 1958, when Letha Cavendish Greene, a beautiful, calm woman with an unforgettable voice, widowed for eight years, decided she must sell the *Delta Queen*.

It was a moment of desperation. There seemed to be no other way to turn. The daughter-in-law of the Petticoat Skipper, a woman dedicated to boats and rivers herself, and her four children with her, she still could not continue to operate the river boat at such a loss.

The *Delta Queen* was advertised for sale. If there were no buyers, she would be sold as junk and cut up for scrap.

II. *It Was the Children Who Saved the Queen*

The news hit the newspapers, the radio and river journals. As with an electric shock, America read that the *Delta Queen* had actually been put up for sale. Only a comparatively few people in America had ever heard of the river boat, much less had had a ride on her, though her former California passengers never forgot their favorite craft, and her mid-continent passengers were faithful to her memory. There just were not enough of them to keep her afloat.

But no matter that most people did not know the *Delta Queen*. They were awakened to the fact that here was the very last overnight passenger steamboat, a luxury liner of the inland rivers, about to be sold to an unknown fate. And if there were no buyers—after all, who would want a big steamboat that was steadily losing money?—no one knew what awful fate might befall her.

Many desperate plans were put forth, were pondered, discarded. *How to save the* Queen? In Cincinnati, Memphis, Louisville, St. Louis, Pittsburgh and other cities along the rivers, as well as in Chicago, earnest people were trying to solve the problem of rescuing the Big Lady before it was too late. *Before it was too late* . . . and the time was fast running out. People who had never heard of the *Delta Queen* knew about her now. She had made the newspapers from New York to San Francisco. People who had thought little if anything of the Mississippi or the Ohio Rivers were aware that a steamboat still traveled those rivers, and passengers could ride her as in Mark Twain's day, or at least they could as long as this priceless vessel was permitted to continue in existence.

Men tried, cities tried, but it was the children who saved the *Queen*.

Margaret, Richard, Robert and Mary, the four children of Mr. and Mrs. Richard Simonton of Los Angeles, had taken a trip on the *Delta Queen* during the summer before. They had been enchanted with the wonderful experience. It had brought to them the romance of what Mark Twain had been talking about, had shown them what the country looks like from the deck of a river boat; and they had had such a glorious time that they wanted to do it again. When the 1958 schedule arrived, they all decided to take the cruise to Reelfoot Lake in June.

On a day in January, shortly after their reservations were sent in, the blow fell.

"Listen to this," said Richard Simonton, a letter and a check in his hand. "I've had word from the Greene Line that the trip on the *Delta Queen* is off. We won't be going on a river boat this summer. In fact, I don't suppose we ever will again, or anyone else, either. They've put the boat up for sale!"

"Oh, no, they can't!" exclaimed Margaret, who was thirteen. "Not our beautiful, beautiful *Delta Queen!*"

"What a mess!" cried Dick, eleven. He went over to read the letter himself, to make sure his father had read it right.

Robert, eight, and Mary, five, just sat with unhappy faces.

"Well, I know you're sorry about it, and so am I," protested their father. "But what do you expect *me* to do about it?"

"But think of it, Daddy!" they cried. "Oh, can't we do *something?*"

Richard Simonton never thought he would come to spend hours musing over a great white steamboat with a red and white stern wheel and a financial problem as big as her 285-foot length. After the children had hurried off to school that day and he had gone to his office, he couldn't keep his mind away from the situation. He wasted time at his desk, drummed his fingers, looked out of the window at the hot California sunshine. What he saw was not California, but a white steamer tied up to an Ohio River shore, then a big stern wheel slowly revolving and casting silver drops back into the muddy waters of the river. This lovely picture always became replaced with a more disagreeable one, the horrid vision of the freshly painted, elegant *Delta Queen* under the ruthless hammers and torches and dismantling cranes of the wreckers, her steel being sliced up for scrap. And that was too much to bear!

That was when an idea hit him.

He made a long-distance telephone call to his friend, Jay Quinby, at Summit, New Jersey.

"Jay, this is Dick—Dick Simonton," he began when the call was put through. "No, I'm not in New York; still out in

California and the weather's fine and warm. Listen, Jay," he went on, "did you hear about that steamer, the *Delta Queen*, over at Cincinnati, the one we rode last year, being put up for sale? You did?

"Well, look, you used to be interested in steamboats and your son is an engineer and crazy about boats, too. Why don't we three get together and buy the controlling interest in that vessel? That way, we'd be sure of having a steamboat handy when we want one; my kids'll be happy; and we'd have done a good thing for everybody. And I believe that, with the right kind of advertising, we could make that boat into a paying proposition."

Jay Quinby, an electronics engineer, had played the calliope long ago on the Ohio River steamer *Lulu Belle*, at Huntington, West Virginia, and had been in love with rivers and steamboats ever since. He and his son Jack got together with Dick Simonton, and, while a nation which had become newly river-conscious watched, they became the new owners of the *Delta Queen*. Once more she had brushed death and extinction, and had survived.

Things would go on much as before, with Letha Greene as general manager and president of the line, with her eldest daughter, Mary Greene Cleary, as social director, and Mary's husband, Jack Cleary, as steward. Young Gordon Greene II filled a night watchman's post during his summer vacation from law school. Much of the same crew would remain, headed by Captain Paul Underwood as master. Most of the same maids and waiters and deck crew who had been with the Greene Line for many years would continue. Everything would be the same, but with a difference.

The publicity which had covered the country during those tension-filled days in January and February, when the fate of an Ohio River boat was unknown, when no one knew what was going to happen to the *Delta Queen* and river history, had built up an eager following, although many of these people had never even heard of the *Queen* before and had no great interest in river history. There was no more trouble, now, with a too-meager passenger list, not with Jay Quinby spreading his advertising over the country, not with people in river towns vowing they would not let another year go by without riding the *Queen*. The 1958 cruises were sold out.

And so the *Delta Queen*, saved from extinction on the scrap heap, or from becoming a static wharf boat, or a floating restaurant or museum, is moored at the Greene Line Steamers dock once again, waiting to load passengers for the next cruise down the wonderful, ever-changing, never-changing, exciting rivers of mid-America.

Winter had seemed very long and unusually cold, even in the far South, where the orange trees had been injured by the great freeze, and ice had extended almost down to Memphis. In the northern part of the Mississippi Valley, there had been more snow than anyone could remember for a long, long time. Hay had been flown to marooned cattle and horses in the blizzard-swept Dakotas, and icebreakers had to escort tows of barges in convoy up the Illinois River to Chicago. A long, hard winter for everyone . . . until, on a somewhat milder day in early March, the first robin appeared on a thawed patch of lawn beside a city street. If robins were back, then surely, surely, spring would not be long in coming!

A week later, a fresh snow came down, wet and sticky and thick, heaping itself heavily on trees and roofs, half-burying cars along the streets of Cincinnati, blocking highways in Illinois, submerging Wisconsin even deeper than it had been all winter. But this was a Robin Snow, wet and transient. Down along the Ohio River, it began to melt by the next day and poured streams of snow water into every creek and ditch and river. And down the Ohio came floating the last of the

Monongahela ice, the last frigid evidences of winter.

Crocuses came up through the vestiges of snow. Blue scillas cast patches of sky-color on soggy brown earth. Skunk cabbages sent up brown-purple cornucopias out of half-frozen swamps, and the open oak woods suddenly came alive in a drifting of white and pink spring beauties . . . when the sun came out at last.

The sun at last! Flowers at last! Bluebirds on fence posts and robins on lawns! Maples blooming and pussy willows fluffing! It was surely spring now, surely it must be, for April was close at hand and the surge of life and growth and urgency was all about, only waiting for a little warmth, a little more sunshine, a little encouragement, to become a full-blown spring.

It seemed to me that I had been waiting a year for winter to end. In February, when I knew that I would take a steamboat ride in April, it only intensified the severity of winter to know that so many weeks lay between me and the fulfillment of adventure.

The snow went, the daffodil buds showed color, the brown thrashers were back. I packed a suitcase and didn't forget my camera and binoculars, nor the dark glasses against the sun I felt certain would be dazzling in the South. And on a lowering, grim, chill and rainy day I boarded a train for Cincinnati.

The train traveled north for a hundred miles before changing to a more southern route, but, in that space of time and landscape, spring visibly retreated. All greenery was gone, all the look of springtime. Rain swept in an unrelenting gray sheet across the sodden stubblefields where the little horned larks flitted.

But by the time the train had slanted into Indiana, slanted southeast into Ohio, and reached Cincinnati, the rain was misting upon weeping willows glowing with green; pink

Japanese magnolias were in bloom, and forsythia made masses of gold along the river parkways. Somewhere down below the city buildings, somewhere out of sight beside the broad Ohio River, a steamboat waited for me to come aboard. Next day—next day adventure would begin!

12. Adventure into Springtime

By morning, the sky had cleared and the April sun was gay and bright in a cold wind as I hurried aboard the *Delta Queen*, where she lay at the Greene Lines wharf boat in Cincinnati. I settled my things in my stateroom and then hastily came out on deck to watch the procedure of loading and embarking. In a few hours, the big steamer would set off on her first cruise of the new season, a journey 2,700 miles in length, round trip, from Cincinnati, Ohio, to New Orleans, Louisiana.

At one o'clock in the afternoon, on a Saturday in early April, the *Delta Queen's* big red paddle wheel was lazily turning over, the water drops splashing from plank to plank and finally spilling silver back into the green-brown liquid of the Ohio River. A small amount of black smoke breathed from the big chimney standing on the roof, just back of the pilothouse. The great white boat had an air of readiness, almost an eagerness to set off again after a winter of inactivity, to navigate the river waters in the newborn springtime of the year.

On a short shake-down cruise the night before, to test the engines, the pilots had also tested the steering levers, had checked the radio telephone and the bell signals to the engine room, had flipped the big windshield wipers to make sure they worked across the broad front windows, had adjusted the calendar to April.

Today was the day! On the sundeck, on the texas, and on the cabin deck, set in layer-cake style below the roof and the pilothouse, the maids were finishing their bed-making in ninety-seven staterooms. Arrangements of flowers arrived from a florist's shop. Corsages and bouquets—roses, carnations, daffodils, vivid Japanese anemones, gaudy bird-of-paradise blooms—came aboard the steamer, along with boxes of candy, baskets of fruit and other gifts for the passengers.

Bob McCann, the purser, in his little office on the cabin deck, was worriedly wishing that the head office on the wharf boat just across the way would hurry and send him the passenger list. He and the bookkeeper wanted to get the early arrivals situated in their staterooms before the big rush began. Captain Paul Underwood, in his crisp blue serge uniform and white cap, was greeting old friends.

On the lower deck, where the short landing stage connected the boat itself with the big Greene Line wharf boat, Negro deck hands were sitting about on timberheads or stairs, or were tilted back in various attitudes of relaxation in their chairs, some playing cards, some dozing, waiting for the moment to go into action. Several deck hands sat on timberheads at the edge of the wharf boat itself, each one beside a big manila line securing the *Delta Queen* to her landing.

Down the cobbled waterfront of Cincinnati streamed a

steady procession of taxicabs. They drove into the duskiness of the wharf boat to let off passengers and luggage where porters waited, then turned about to race up the steep landing again. Passengers who had come in their own cars, some from as far away as Oregon, Washington, California and New York, parked their vehicles in the wharf boat where they would be awaiting them on the return of the *Delta Queen*, almost three weeks later.

Meanwhile, waiters down in the big, airy dining room were setting tables. Good smells were beginning to issue up the vents from the galley, below in the hold. Most of the *Delta Queen's* crew of seventy had much to do, and they were doing it quietly and efficiently.

In the big, hot, noisy, immaculate engine room, part of it on the first deck but most of the machinery in the hold, the chief engineer and the oilers were making last-minute examinations of the intricate array of generators, pumps, gauges, and switches. The boilers were getting up steam from hot Diesel fires. The carpenter went out on the fantail, from which rose the big stern wheel, twenty-eight feet in diameter and thirty-five feet wide. A bolt had come loose, no one knew how, and must be fixed before the vessel was ready to go. And the time was nearing that zero moment when the *Delta Queen* would separate herself and her passengers from land, would become a little world of her own as she navigated the big rivers, down to springtime in the far South.

Little enough of that new season was visible from where the big boat lay alongside the Cincinnati shore. The landing slanted up from the water to the busy streets and the old red brick structures that had been there for many generations and had seen many steamboats come and go. Above rose the steeps of Mount Washington and Mount Adams and Mount Auburn, hills ranging like mountains around the curve of the river, topped by the bright bowl of the April sky.

The Cincinnati skyline was dramatic and full of splendor between hills and river, yet the river front itself lacked the great line-up of steamboats which once had lain there waiting for passengers. Only the *Delta Queen* was there today, accompanied by small motorboats and other pleasure craft, by an excursion boat called the *Chaperon*, used for short day or evening trips, and by the passing Diesel towboats. The *Gordon C. Greene* was gone, sold to a man in Florida. The *Island Queen* was gone, burned tragically a few years ago. The *Cincinnati* was gone, now known as the *President* down at New Orleans. They were all gone, all but the *Delta Queen*. She alone was left to maintain the unbroken line of steamboats which had traveled the Ohio and the Mississippi.

The short-trip excursion boats at many a river port—the *Avalon*, the *Memphis Queen II*, the *President*, the *Admiral*—are proof that, although the Steamboat Era may have passed away officially, in fact, it still lives in this revived river age, and in the hearts of all of us who find in river travel a pleasant satisfaction.

We are the ones who have grown up with Mark Twain, with his nostalgic stories of the Mississippi in a romantic era which can never come again—and perhaps we wouldn't like it so well if it did! Nevertheless, just about everyone who has read *Huckleberry Finn, Tom Sawyer* and *Life on the Mississippi* seems to possess a certain fascination and awe of the river and its boats.

On that day in April, therefore, passengers were coming from many parts of the country, were coming with eagerness to travel on a leisurely stern-wheeler down a muddy river. To recreate in their own minds and experiences some of the tales they had read, to become part of the old, lost Steamboat Era, to become part of the river and its fascinating ancient past— this was why they had come. And they had a glow in their eyes, anticipating what lay before them, even though many were world travelers.

The excitement was heightened by the bright sunshine and the cold spring wind. Strangers smiled at strangers. The informality of the steamboat put everybody suddenly at ease, gave them a certain joy they might have forgotten.

It was 1:45 P.M. Everything was in order. The passengers who were leaning on the railing of the texas deck were jolted out of their composure by the sudden astounding booming of the big bell, which actually shook the decks with its vibration. Twelve times it tolled, slowly, powerfully. Its ponderous clapper was controlled by a rope passing down through the deck, through the promenade of the cabin deck below, to the foredeck. Here Doc Carr, the second mate, a red bandana tied rakishly around his elderly neck, though otherwise he was dressed in correct Navy-blue serge and a cap which said MATE in gold embroidery, pulled valiantly.

Events began to move faster. With some difficulty, Mrs. Greene's car was brought aboard, for she would get off at Louisville the next day and could thus drive home in a few hours. Mr. Jay Quinby, who had come from New Jersey to see his boat off on her first voyage of the season, decided to remain aboard, too, until the next day, thus putting off his reluctant return to the East. Tall, genial Jay Quinby, in his big tan Stetson and western tie declared wistfully that he would like nothing better than to stay on for the whole trip.

The waiting deck hands got their lines loosed. Captain Underwood, standing with his megaphone on the texas deck, leaned over the railing and supervised the casting off. The short stage was pulled in. The captain bellowed at Will Holloway, head deckhand, affectionately known as Little Willie, and at Gray-Eye, a new deck hand of utmost slowness, to step lively, pull in those lines—*move!* They were all good friends, but the noisy activity, minus the red-hot profanity of an earlier day, looked good to the passengers.

The second mate tolled the bell again, nine times. From the loud-speaker came the pleasant voice of the purser:

"All ashore who are going ashore. The *Delta Queen* is now preparing to leave Cincinnati!"

In the voice of this man whose life is the rivers, there was a special note of anticipation that made it sound as if we and the *Delta Queen* were about to take off on high adventure, to explore the vast unknown spaces of the American wilderness, to discover new shores and exciting lands. Bob McCann has set off on many a steamboat trip. He has worked on boats since he was a youth; it is nothing new and yet it is always new to him. He has a quality of enthusiasm which makes each trip, each casting off, each departure from any port, no matter how grubby, into something thrilling which is happening now for the first time.

Pilot Albert Kelly pulled the whistle handle and a huge, deep-throated, sonorous blast emerged visibly in the puff of steam from the pipes back of the pilothouse roof. One blast, another blast, another, long, loud, and leisurely, with time between each one for the lovely echoes to express themselves against the Cincinnati buildings and then more faintly from the distant hills. Then two shorts, and one long—a tremendous shout of farewell which sent a flurry of pigeons upward in alarm from a warehouse roof.

Suddenly, there was open water between the *Delta Queen* and the wharf boat, where a group of people waving goodby were gradually growing smaller and less distinct. It didn't seem as if the *Queen* were moving at all, but rather that the shore was receding. The big wheel churned faster, kicking white water, dipping deeply into the green-brown Ohio.

The *Queen* moved upstream toward the upper bridge, for a steamboat heads into her mooring on shore with her nose against the current; now she needed to turn about to go

downstream. Slowly, she curved in midstream, her wheel throwing spray that caught sunlight and made a rainbow . . . turned, got squared away. With two more long, triumphant toots of the big whistle, the downbound *Delta Queen* headed majestically under the old Cincinnati suspension bridge.

Cars on shore and bridge blew an answering chorus on their horns. Seeing the *Delta Queen* is always an event. Everyone salutes her with a special kind of wondering affection that she should be there at all. Photographers on the green levee of the Kentucky side took pictures of the passing steamboat against the striking Cincinnati skyline, while, back of her, the red roofs on the hills, lit by the afternoon sun, fell farther and farther behind and then were hidden beyond a bend of the river. The first voyage of the year had begun!

By the time the *Delta Queen* was out of sight of Cincinnati, and by the time she had saluted three passing towboats and had sailed by a succession of little Kentucky towns where peach trees were in bloom and wild plum blossoms cast a drifting of white along the edges of the woods, everyone on board had settled down. Steamer chairs were occupied. The purser had been asked at least a dozen questions about the monument marking President William Henry Harrison's grave on the right bank, and a misplaced stateroom key and a lost glove had been found. There was a fine swish of water past the bows, and the big paddle wheel tossed cool spray into the chill wind.

The *Delta Queen* appeared to be proceeding rapidly down the river. Just how rapidly was difficult to compute, until we watched the mileage markers on shore, every five miles or so. Then it was even more difficult to realize that we were "racing" down the river at the astonishing pace of about sixteen miles an hour. It wasn't possible! Yet speed on the river is different from on shore. Sixteen miles an hour for a steamboat is fast, especially when compared with the five to eight miles an hour which she would make coming back up against the river current, bucking the spring rise.

And the leisurely tempo of river and steamboat laid their gentle hands upon us who had come from the feverish pace of the land, and within a few hours the passing pageant of the river and its gentle life had claimed us. The motion of the boat was smooth and so level that we needed to look at the moving shores to make certain we were actually progressing down the stream.

The dinner chimes sounded, and in the warm, softly lighted, handsome dining room, with its white-coated waiters and its music and its flowers and the delicious dinner, the river and its shores vanished. We could hardly believe we were really traveling on the water, or, in fact, that we were moving any-where. Only the slightest vibration in the Siamese ironbark floor proved the fact. After dinner, there was a get-together party and a dance in the dining room, while, outside, the silent shores and the sibilant voice of the river and the piping of frogs in a marsh, seemed remote from the light and gaiety within.

13. Waterfall in the River

On a bright spring Sunday morning, the *Delta Queen* tied up to the great iron mooring rings set in the stones of the hard, unhandsome, somewhat littered waterfront of Louisville, Kentucky, so that passengers might go to church.

Like many another river town, Louisville has turned its back on the river, and only the factories, the old brick tenements, the breweries and other unlovely structures were visible, while all the beauty of Louisville, its landscaped gardens and parks, its city streets and blossoming trees, were somewhere back, away from a river which has ravaged these shores too often for much permanent beautification to take root.

There was a time, long, long ago, when the Louisville waterfront was frequently as far as a steamboat could go. Vessels bound below had to wait until the water was high enough to carry them over that great obstruction nearby, the rocky cascades known as the Falls of the Ohio. Passengers and freight were carried by oxcart from above the falls, over land, to below, where another steamboat waited to load them and carry them on to points down the Ohio and the Mississippi. It was seldom that a boat could expect to go straight up or downstream, except when the water was very high, for the Ohio could rise rapidly and fall twice as fast. During a large part of each year, most of it was quite unnavigable.

The presence of the falls created a natural stopping place for boats of all sorts, from the canoes of Indians and the flatboats and rafts of pioneers, to the first steamboats attempting to navigate this unpredictable stream. As part of a line of defense against the Indians during the days of the American Revolution, George Rogers Clark built a fort on an island in the middle of the river, above the falls. Seeking this protection, a number of settlers came to live there. Then, long before the island was swept away by the river, Clark moved to the mainland and built another fort where Louisville now stands. Around it rose more and more cabins of pioneers, forming the nucleus of a town.

Each year, when the water was low and the falls impassable, a certain number of travelers landed with their goods to wait for the water to rise and float their craft over the falls. Some stayed so long that they planted gardens and put up cabins—and just decided to stay where they were, instead of building elsewhere. Or perhaps because of illness some could not go on when the river rose. So for one reason or another, the voyagers became attached to the spot. It was George Rogers Clark who actually founded Louisville, but it was the Falls of the Ohio which was responsible for much of the early population. They came, they waited, they stayed.

But, although the falls offer a hindrance to navigation, these rocky cascades have been an aid to men and animals in crossing the river from bank to bank, from Kentucky to

Indiana, ever since the mammoths crossed to the salt licks in northern Kentucky, a million years ago. The ledge of rock forming the falls was made of Niagara limestone, jutting from the river bottom, an old coral reef left from Silurian seas four hundred million years ago. During high water, the ledges were concealed, but in low water creatures could cross without getting wet above their knees. This was the ford of the old Buffalo Trace, the place where the Warriors' Path went over, a vital part of the trail which became one of the important pioneer highways in America, leading west to the Mississippi.

The rocks in the river may have been a great help to those wishing to cross on foot, but they were always a bother to boats. Finally, in 1825, private interests decided to do something about the situation which was tying up commerce on this important watery highway connecting the Ohio with the markets of the South. A canal was planned which would bypass the falls on the Louisville side and open the bottleneck. So, laboriously and slowly a small canal and lock were dug. Completed in 1830, the Portland Canal charged a toll for every type of vessel passing through, at a rate based on the number of tons of freight. Although rivermen grumbled, they were thankful to get around the falls at any price. The canal owners prospered.

Less than ten years after it was in operation, more than 1,500 steamboats and hundreds of keelboats and flatboats had gone through the canal and lock. Traffic was rapidly growing as the navigability of the Ohio was proved. It was not long before everyone using the Portland Canal knew that it had quite outgrown the amount of traffic crowding into it. The canal was almost as much a hindrance as the falls had been.

The canal was rebuilt, and rebuilt again, and could never quite keep up with the increasing steamboat traffic, nor the growing size of the boats and tows, especially in that period more than a hundred years after the first canal was built, when enormous coal and oil tows and large Diesel boats came to the busy Ohio.

And so the Louisville-Portland Canal once more was being widened and enlarged on this April day when the *Delta Queen* moved away from the Louisville waterfront. Instead of going directly between the guide-walls of the canal, the pilot of the *Delta Queen* navigated her over to the side to wait.

Ahead, on the starboard bank, there was a sudden dull boom, and a fountain of sand and debris shot into the air. A charge of dynamite had been set off in that endless process of widening the canal which seems to go on forever. No sooner had the *Delta Queen* started off again and moved into the narrow confines of the canal than she halted once more. The highway bridge at Louisville had been easy enough to pass beneath but the railroad bridge, built far too low across the canal itself, had not opened to let her through.

The pilot pulled the whistle handle, pulled long and hard. The bridge did not stir. The *Queen* nudged over against the canal wall, waiting. The wind blew an extra puff and shoved her dangling landing stage into the trees, sheering off part of a young cottonwood and scattering its red, caterpillarlike catkins on the stage and deck. The pilot blew again . . . and still the bridge remained closed. At last, the cause of the delay, a leisurely freight train, began inching at a turtle's pace across the span.

Trains have priority on bridges, and, if one is coming, the boats must wait, no matter how slow the train. This one moved to the middle of the bridge, paused . . . then began slowly to back up . . . then inched forward. A train has the power to hold up a boat for hours, and a good many rivermen feel bitterly certain that the railroad men do it on purpose to infuriate them.

There was once a bridge tender at this very structure

across the Louisville-Portland Canal who had an intense dislike for boats. He always hated to open the bridge for them. He felt that river traffic was an imposition and an insult to the railroads, and the bridge shouldn't have to be opened and closed at the whim of every whistle-tooting upstart vessel wanting to go through.

So one day the tender didn't open the span. A towboat blew and blew and got no results. Other boats pulled up to wait also, on both sides of the bridge. Hours went by and it didn't open. Finally, the captain of the first boat got off and walked up to find out what had happened, thinking maybe the bridge tender was ill or had gone home.

But he was there. He was sitting with his feet propped up, reading the afternoon paper and drinking coffee. He seemed unrepentant when the towboat pilot insisted that the bridge be opened.

"Well, you can't help unavoidable circumstances," said the bridge man. "I guess it'll open whenever we get ready to open it."

The towboat captain was sizzling when he went back to his boat. There was nothing he could do but continue to wait until, finally, the bridge did open—six hours later. But when that first boat got exactly under it, blocking the opening, the captain ordered the crew to tie up to the pier and wait.

The bridge tender was alarmed. There was a train due in half an hour and another an hour after that. And he couldn't close the span until that boat was out from under, not to mention all the others who were waiting to go through.

"What's happened down there?" he called worriedly to the captain, who was sitting calmly in his pilothouse, placidly eating an apple. "Why don't you move out so I can close my bridge?"

"Well, you can't help unavoidable circumstances, can you?" asked the captain innocently, tossing his core into the river.

"I guess the boat'll move on when it gets ready. And all the others behind me. Unless *they* decide to stop here, too."

There he stayed for another hour, giving plenty of time for the lesson to sink in, while the train was held up, and the bridge tender was about ready to burst with rage.

That was the last time he delayed a towboat. After that, at the first whistle up ahead, the bridge swung open, fast!

And it finally opened for the *Delta Queen*. When the train had crawled across and was on its way, the span turned and opened, and the river boat moved ahead and into the lock chamber whose open gates were waiting.

It was a snug fit for such a large craft. The lock chamber is fifty-eight feet wide and the *Delta Queen's* width is fifty-six feet. That leaves little room to spare, but it was enough. The lock gates closed, and we could see how the wet brown lock walls appeared to be rising higher and higher as the boat sank and the water was pumped out. The *Queen* was lowered twenty-four feet in the chamber, down to the level of the river below the Falls of the Ohio which she was thus neatly bypassing. The falls lay somewhere to the right, but no one aboard could see them, hear their cascading power, or realize their menace. Finally, the *Delta Queen* moved smoothly out of the lower part of the chamber of Lock 41 and left the Louisville-Portland Canal for the open waters of the Ohio.

There is only one waterfall on the Ohio, but there are many bridges, and they have always plagued river boats. The fact that it was the railroads which built the bridges has made matters even worse, for between railroads and steamboats there was a bitter contest for the nation's passengers and freight.

The railroads argued that boats were necessarily restricted to the rivers. If one wished to travel by boat, he had to travel by ways of the dictating watercourses, and these did not always lead to where he wanted to go. The railroads, however, extending their network farther and farther in all directions, could serve the nation far better. For many years, however, steamboats on the Mississippi had taken care of the north-south traffic. The business interests of St. Louis and New Orleans were theirs. The railroads held the east-west routes, controlled by Chicago and New York. And the contest grew as the nation grew. The steamboats boasted they could go anywhere that water went. There were some which had only a nine-inch draft, so they could navigate through a flooded cornfield or, as their owners proudly boasted, could "float on a heavy dew."

A railroad, however, much as it might wander over the landscape, was not aquatic. When it came to a river, a railroad stopped. For some time, in fact, the rail lines ended right there at the water's edge, for there were no bridges. Ferry service took care of hauling passengers and freight over the river, where they might get aboard another train on the other side. It was a good deal the same situation as the one the old steamboats had found at the Falls of the Ohio, and just as much of a nuisance.

In 1855, the Rock Island Railroad proposed to build a bridge across the Mississippi between Rock Island, Illinois, and Davenport, Iowa. This would end the bothersome transfer of train passengers and tons of freight by the ferries— which would undoubtedly cry out at having their business taken away. But the railroad *must* have a bridge.

It was not only the ferries which protested, though. From the steamboat people of the Mississippi there arose a concerted objection, a cry of horror and rebellion. Bridges would be the ruination of steamboat traffic! It was a conspiracy of railroad interests to destroy steamboating! Bridges would bar boats, would wreck vessels, would restrict many by not letting them get under the spans during high water. This is a battle which has never ended. Today, a similar discussion goes on whenever a new bridge is proposed to cross a navigable river.

The Rock Island Railroad built its bridge. The company ignored the lawsuits that were simmering and the endless protests of the rivermen. And the following year, the steamboat *Effie Afton*, a side-wheeler carrying a heavy load of passengers, freight and a number of oxen, miscalculated the distance going under the bridge and rammed hard on a stone support. The boat caught fire and sank, and part of the bridge span burned. Many people died in the disaster, and the oxen, badly injured and bawling in agony, got to shore and charged madly in pain-filled panic through the bottomland woods.

In spite of the calamity which had happened to one of their kind, the steamboatmen up and down the Mississippi openly rejoiced at this justification of what they had predicted would happen, and which must continue to happen as long as a bridge remained, they declared. Passing steamboats saluted the wrecked span with derisive and insulting whistles.

The company which owned the *Effie Afton* sued the Rock Island Railroad. A prominent lawyer, Abraham Lincoln of Springfield, Illinois, was selected to defend the bridge and its owners. The case was tried in Chicago.

Lincoln, at heart still a riverman, was careful in planning his case. He went to Rock Island and hired a rowboat in which he floated under the bridge, around the bridge, studying currents and line of drift. He made inquiries and found out that the starboard wheel of the *Effie Afton* had been out of commission at the time of the accident, which would naturally have caused the pilot to aim poorly in passing beneath the bridge. Back in Chicago, he presented his arguments skillfully.

"One man has as good a right to cross a river as another has to sail up or down it. . . . This bridge must be treated with respect in this court, and is not to be kicked about with contempt. . . . The proper mode for all parties in this affair is to 'live and let live.' "

The jury was so much divided in opinion by this time that it could not come to any decision. With a hung jury, the case was dismissed. But it was considered to be a victory for railroads and their bridges.

With the Rock Island bridge rebuilt, others, one by one, began to cross the Mississippi and the Ohio. In the face of public distrust and some of the heaviest currents in the river, James Eads built the great bridge across the Mississippi at St. Louis. And every now and again, even today, a steamboat or a towboat rams into a bridge support, or into the bridge itself, in time of high water. The problem which was so acute a hundred years ago is still serious today.

That was why, when the *Delta Queen* came to the inland rivers, her chimney had to be cut down and hinged so that it could be put back out of the way for clearance. A hinged smokestack was nothing new. To the old-time steamboats with their enormously tall chimneys, it was necessary after the bridges were built. But even with hinged smokestacks and lower pilothouses, high water made some bridges impossible to pass.

The bridges on the Ohio River are an annual problem to the bulky height of the *Delta Queen*. In March, 1955, on her way back from the Mardi Gras trip, the *Queen* squeaked under the Louisville bridge by a scant twelve inches, even with the eight-foot extension removed from the chimney. The river was so high that the *Delta Queen* could navigate over the Falls of the Ohio as she came upstream; and only once before had she done it, going down.

Then, after all the trouble she had on this return trip, the steamer could not get under the bridge close to her home port, could not reach Cincinnati. Ignominiously, she had to unload her passengers on the Kentucky shore, where they were taken by taxicab to the city.

In May, 1958, the *Queen* met high water once more, so high that she couldn't get to her own wharf boat but had to have her passengers brought to her at Ludlow, Kentucky. On their way at last, Captain Underwood met another old and enduring aggravation, that Louisville highway bridge again!

Paul Underwood is a man of experience and wisdom on the rivers, so he decided he would get under the bridge and do it safely. First he took on a full load of fuel oil and then added a considerable tonnage of water as further ballast. He took off the *Queen's* smokestack extension; he removed even the whistle because it stuck above the pilothouse a little way. He would have taken off the pilothouse itself if he could.

Then Captain Underwood started the boat backward down the river, pointing the *Delta Queen's* landing stage upstream, running her engines full speed ahead, yet navigating backward, thus cutting the big boat's actual speed until it almost equalled that of the current. Down in the engine room, the chief engineer followed the indicator signals expertly with the throttle. The two of them eased that big steamboat carefully down to the bridge, yet were on trigger-sharp alertness to send the *Queen* back upstream if she wasn't going to *quite* clear the obstruction.

A crewman climbed up close to the top of the pilothouse and held up a ruler, to see if there was going to be any clearance at all . . . and there was: seven or eight inches, but that was enough.

People on shore held their breaths as the *Delta Queen,* appearing to be swept against her will backward down the river, to be wrecked on the bridge, saw her slide under safely without crashing, after all. Once below the bridge, the resourceful river boat, in quiet triumph, rounded and headed down the river again on the rolling, tumbling, racing floodwater.

Just below were the Falls of the Ohio. The usual thirty-five-foot drop, which is much less in low water, is taken care of by the lock at Dam Number 41, but there was no need for the lock this time. Tops of trees were sticking out of the flood on both banks, so the *Delta Queen* navigated at high speed down the cascades, "shooting the chutes" with aplomb—and causing considerable excitement for all on board.

Some steamboats were not as lucky as the *Queen* in getting under bridges. Another *Queen* didn't quite make it. As a news writer in the Gallipolis *Daily Tribune* said on March 8, 1899:

> "The *Queen City* departed for Pittsburgh this morning, and the wind was whistling through the whiskers of the pilot, owing to the pilothouse roof being off."

This laconic comment was aroused because the pilot hadn't *quite* judged his clearance of the bridge at Kenova, West Virginia. The *Queen City* was one of the river's finest packets during the latter portion of the Steamboat Era, perishing at last in 1933. The bell of this fine boat is the one now used on the *Delta Queen*.

It was in March that the *Queen City* was moving upriver with a heavy load of freight and passengers. The stream was rising rapidly from storms in the hills and the runoff of snows in Pennsylvania, and the wind was blowing full force, as if winter were coming back again. The Ohio had reached the dangerous stage of forty-eight feet before the captain and the pilot knew what had happened in the wild black night.

The captain struggled outside in the gale and climbed up to the top of the pilothouse, to see what clearance there was under the Kenova bridge. He could barely make out the dim shape of the structure up ahead, and it seemed to him that it was going to come mighty close to the height of the pilothouse. Before he could decide anything further, there was a crash in the wind and darkness, the sound of desperately splintering wood. The captain tumbled down into the wreckage of what had been the pilothouse of the *Queen City*. There had been no clearance at all under that bridge, and the roof had been sheared off.

The wreckage pinned the pilot, Tony Meldahl, between the big wheel and the pilothouse wall. A wire lashed across his neck, and he struggled to get away from it before it strangled him. No one at all was steering the *Queen City*, which had passed under the bridge and now raced blindly on through the night.

The pilot struggled, and the wire snapped. He could breathe again! He pushed aside the splintered wreckage and dug out the injured captain. Captain Meldahl took hold of the wheel and rang the engine room to slow down. A crewman hurried upstairs to see what had happened. He had difficulty wrenching the door open and was aghast when he saw the ruin inside. But Captain Meldahl had the boat under control and, as the news writer said:

"The wind was whistling through the whiskers of the pilot, owing to the pilothouse roof being off."

All this was in the past—yet not too far away for the possibility of its happening again. But on this fine, chilly, spring day, the *Delta Queen* proceeded at a fast clip on a rising river down the Ohio. Bridge by bridge, she would pass under each when the time came.

14. General Lafayette's Steamboat Wreck

The *Delta Queen* sailed calmly over the spot where General Lafayette nearly lost his life in a steamboat wreck. Located a few miles below Louisville and the Falls of the Ohio, this might have been the scene of a national disgrace, for Lafayette was a beloved hero, a guest of the United States, and if anything had happened to him, the world would never have forgiven America. His hosts and countless people along the route he took in touring the country were appalled at what had almost been permitted to happen to America's favorite foreign hero, who stood beside the revered George Washington as a saviour of the land.

Lafayette's visit to America in 1824–25, after such a long time away, had become a triumphal procession, lasting a year. He, Marie Joseph Paul Roch Yves Gilbert Motier, the Marquis de Lafayette had come back to his adored America— and America loved him for it.

In the days of the American Revolution, Lafayette had been a youth of twenty. He was handsome, impetuous, with an outgoing personality which made him liked by everyone with whom he had contact, from soldiers in the ranks to the highest officials, such as Washington and Jefferson. He had materially aided our fight for independence, and his own fierce dedication to freedom for all men radiated almost like an aura around him. The Indians had recognized that look; so had great men and small, in many places and circumstances. That noble motive had almost cost him his life during the French Revolution, but he had survived all assaults of his enemies. And to remind himself of America, he had named his son Georges Washington and his daughter Virginie.

Everyone knew of Lafayette's exploits. He had become history. Schoolboys of several generations had grown up with his story. It seemed incredible now that this almost legendary hero, nearly half a century later, should still be alive, still devoted to America, and that he should come back for a friendly personal visit to the country which revered his name.

It was to be an extensive, leisurely tour. He would not only renew friendships in the East, which included pretty much of the civilized part of America when he was there in 1777, but he would travel out to St. Louis, the farthest westward point of the growing republic in the year 1825.

For a year he would learn to know America as it had become. He was saddened by the realization that many of his old friends were gone—George Washington, Benjamin Franklin, Paul Revere, Nathanael Greene—the vital, exciting men who had sparked the American Revolution and whose powerful personalities had drawn him here. Now, at sixty-seven, he felt very sure that he would never come back again.

With his son, Georges, and his faithful servant, Bastien, and a secretary, Levasseur, who was to write down all that happened and help to answer his correspondence and deal with people and places, Lafayette at last arrived in New York, on August 14, 1824.

America had never given to any foreigner so wholehearted a welcome and one which lasted so long. Perhaps no other visiting celebrity ever had quite so good a time being entertained, either. Lafayette did not criticize crudities or mistakes; he did not compare American ways with French ways; he only admired all that went well, and knew that it was being done because the people loved him.

It was not until the following February, 1825, when the social season in New York and Washington, at which he had been the lion, seemed to be drawing to an end and spring coming, that Lafayette and his staunch companions set out on the long tour which would take them to the Mississippi and the Ohio. They went a roundabout way, but they got to the rivers at last.

By carriage, they went to Charleston; by sea, to Savannah; by river, to Augusta; and by carriage again, to Montgomery, Alabama. As Lafayette's carriage, with horsemen in escort, entered the wild forest roads of the South, people along the way rushed out to wave and cheer, or else they stood open-mouthed, as if someone straight out of the history books had come to life before their eyes.

When the wilderness route through the southern pines and under the broad-spreading, deeply-shadowed live oaks hung with long, lavender-gray festoons of moss which brushed the carriage, led the party into Indian country, the Cherokees themselves turned out to meet the hero. Tribesmen living along the Chattahoochee River and Uchee Creek suddenly appeared, to stand in respectful silence along the trail. To them, cheering was unseemingly, silence an honor.

They, too, knew of Lafayette. He was the warrior from across the water who, long ago, had come to champion the cause of liberty and who had fought at the side of the Great Father, Washington, to free America from the rule of the Red Coats. The Indians, like the schoolboys, had heard from their fathers about Lafayette, knew that he loved liberty and freedom, knew that he believed in it for all men. They understood that he abhorred slavery and tyranny of any sort. He was their friend.

With silence and ceremony they awaited his coming. The chiefs came to the carriage to greet him and invite him into their houses. There, the head men sat around in solemn respect while he talked. When the procession went on, Indians from one area escorted him to the boundaries of the next, watching jealously to see that no other tribe outdid them in honors. He was not without guards, ever. And when the carriage came to a raging creek which had gone out of its banks from rains up in the mountains, so the bridge was submerged, stalwart Indians waded almost up to their armpits, to stand in two parallel rows, marking where the bridge lay, so that the high-wheeled carriage might pass over safely. In another place, the strong Choctaw braves lifted and carried his vehicle across a washout.

It must have been a strange and unforgettable journey through the southern wilderness, down to Montgomery, where the entertainment was civilized again, though no more wholehearted and affectionate than the hospitality he had received from his brothers of the forest.

At Mobile, Alabama, on the Gulf coast, he boarded a steamboat named the *Natchez,* sent by the Louisiana government to conduct him to the mouth of the Mississippi and up the river to New Orleans, for a rousing welcome by that French city and its emotional Creole inhabitants. To them, he was a precious part of France, the France to which they all felt some-

how inescapably attached and which they might never see again.

But the river called. After a period of rich Gallic entertainment in New Orleans, the indefatigable Lafayette and the three others—Georges, Bastien and Levasseur—set out on their special steamboat, the *Natchez*, up the strong spring current of the Mississippi. It was April 15, 1825, and they were bound for St. Louis. The white side-wheel boat made a stop at Baton Rouge and another at its namesake city of *Natchez*, high on its hill. And then the boat paddled off into what Lafayette must have felt was the true western American wilderness. Natchez was the last civilized outpost until they reached St. Louis.

For thirteen days the boat labored upstream until finally it landed at St. Louis, where the venerable Colonel Auguste Chouteau, who had helped to found the city, met the distinguished guests in his carriage. There was an elaborate party

*Lafayette was the warrior from across the water who, long
ago, had come to champion the cause of liberty.*

and ball at the Chouteau mansion.

Governor Coles of Illinois attended, expressly so that he might invite and persuade Lafayette to come to his state. And the amiable general, who accepted just about all the invitations tendered, and all the gifts, no matter how incongruous—even live geese and fawns—graciously agreed.

So, at midnight, he and the governor set off in the *Natchez* and steamed downriver to Kaskaskia, the old territorial capital and first state capital of Illinois, even then being eaten up by the Mississippi . . . and now long since vanished. Word had been sent ahead by messenger, but he got to Kaskaskia only a short time before the arrival of the steamer. The town was not expecting such eminent guests so soon, and everybody was in a flurry to get ready.

To Lafayette, it didn't matter about the entertainment. He found it much the same in all American towns, and he appreciated all of it because of the honest intentions and friendliness behind it. In Kaskaskia, however, he had a new experience. Here he not only had contact with the French but with Indians again, and Lafayette had always liked Indians.

There was one who interested him especially, a woman of the Algonquin tribe who had been reared and educated in the family of Pierre Menard, first lieutenant governor of Illinois. This woman possessed something which, Lafayette had been told with some secrecy, would greatly stir him. The Indian woman was too shy, however, to come to him. So General Marie Joseph Paul Roch Yves Gilbert Motier, the Marquis de Lafayette, went to see her.

He found her in the servants' quarters behind the house, a white brick building with a big hill rising behind and broad maples shading it. The Indian woman stood with eyes cast down and hands nervously clasped before her. Around her neck hung a small, beautifully fashioned doeskin bag.

"What is it?" asked the old general kindly. "What is it you

wished to show me?"

"Monsieur," she said in a low voice, "my father when he died many years ago gave me this little bag and told me to keep it always. In it is a letter which, he said, would make friends for me among white men wherever I went. He said it was written by one who was greatly honored in America, one from across the water. He said it was written by—you, my lord Lafayette!"

She swiftly took off the bag and opened it, then handed to the astonished marquis a tattered old letter, browned with age, which he himself had written long ago, in Albany, New York, in the year 1784. In it he had thanked a certain Indian chief for his aid and services to the Americans during the war. This had happened such a long, long time ago, in so different a period of history as to seem in another age, not alone in a different century. But the chief had been this Indian woman's father . . . and now here she was, and the letter. He shook his head. It was another one of the strange things which happened in America.

At midnight, after the usual late dinner, toasts and a ball, the *Natchez* set forth again—down the Mississippi and up into the Ohio . . . into the mouth of the Cumberland . . . heading for Nashville, where her honored passenger was to be entertained by Andrew Jackson. After that, Governor Carroll of Tennessee accompanied the boat when she went back to the Ohio. . . . And the next stop, in contrast with the elegance of Nashville, was the pioneer river village of Shawneetown, Illinois, where hogs rooted in the mud streets and most of the waterfront houses were up on stilts.

Shawneetown might not have looked prepossessing, but it was nevertheless the financial and business center of the lower Ohio and of the southern part of Illinois. In the early nineteenth century, most of the state's population was located there. In fact, the place rather looked down its nose at up-

state towns, so that when two men from the struggling village of Chicago, three hundred miles to the north, came all
the way to Shawneetown to ask for a loan of a thousand
dollars, the local bank was reluctant to grant it. Investigators
rode to Chicago, haughtily cast an eye over its mudholes
and dismal houses, then returned south again. The Shawneetown bank refused to loan the money to men from such a
hopeless village as Chicago, which, they felt confident, had
no future.

Bank loans were unimportant, however, in the face of such
news as had reached Shawneetown—the illustrious Lafayette
was coming to visit! But the streets—Chicago wasn't the only
Illinois town afflicted with mud. The mayor had an inspiration: Shawneetown would roll out, not a red carpet, but a
bolt or two of brand-new calico for the general to walk on.

When he stepped down from the landing stage of the
Natchez, the Marquis trod upon clean, new, red and blue
calico, just unwrapped from the bolt, and it stretched all the
way to the balconied, two-story brick hotel, where town
officials were waiting to welcome him. Lafayette inwardly
chuckled. He must remember to tell people at home how
he, Lafayette, had actually promenaded down a length of
sprigged calico, depriving no one knew how many young
ladies of dress material!

There was the usual banquet, accompanied by the usual
toasts and speeches, and Lafayette, having sat through so
many such occasions, let his mind wander and his gaze drift
to the open doorway of the candlelit dining room. He blinked
and looked again. He thought he saw a French soldier, a very
old French soldier in a uniform that was worn and battered.
Yearningly, the apparition gazed at Lafayette, and then the
general remembered. He leaped to his feet while his wine
glass tottered and the mayor stopped in the middle of an interminable speech to stare.

But Lafayette was across the room and had reached the man in the doorway. He had his arms around him, was kissing him on both sunken cheeks, while tears ran down the man's face and down the general's, too.

"Philippe François, *mon ami!*" the general was crying, still embracing the man. "My own good friend and guardian! See, all of you, who it is I have found—the bodyguard who cared well for me during the war, so long ago!"

And in spite of the old man's protests, Lafayette escorted his former bodyguard to a place of honor at the table, before he would allow the proceedings to continue. America! Only in America could such strange things contrive to happen!

Much, much later that night, Lafayette and his party said their farewells and followed the calico path down to the waterfront, where their belongings had been transferred from the steamboat *Natchez* to a smaller boat, the *Mechanic*, already carrying a good many passengers. Rooms had been secured for the visiting general's party, including General Carroll of Tennessee, his escort to Louisville. The *Natchez* blew a farewell whistle and steamed down the river, while the *Mechanic* set off upstream, and Shawneetown fired twenty-four rounds of shot, to the accompaniment of cheers and huzzahs.

Lafayette sank into a chair and sighed. He was finally growing physically weary of the endless succession of speeches, toasts, cheers, dinners, balls and people—so many people. Bastien, clucking his tongue at the tired look on his master's gentle face, helped him to disrobe and got him into bed with a soothing hot toddy. Georges stood and looked down at his father and shook his head.

"Papa, you will kill yourself with so much entertainment," he warned.

"Ah, well, my son," the old man replied, smiling drowsily, "they are all so kind and mean so well. They would not willingly harm a hair of my head and do not really intend to tire me—and was it not wonderful to find Philippe François here in these backwoods? Besides, I take too much pleasure in it all to feel fatigue. But I must confess . . ." And the general, gently snoring, was asleep.

Levasseur busied himself writing up his journal and penning more letters of thanks to be sent to the towns which had entertained the general, while the hours moved on toward midnight. The steady churning of the paddle wheel and the rhythmic throbbing of the engines, the exhaust puffing in the stacks, all this was soothing and pleasant.

Moonlight had made the river clearly visible for night navigation, but soon clouds came up and rain began. The night and the boat and the river were enclosed in the wet blackness of midnight. Instead of tying up, the pilot doggedly kept on, straining to see his way, knowing he was due in Louisville tomorrow with an illustrious guest, so taking a reckless chance in navigating on such a night.

Then the steamboat, suddenly and with no warning, crunched upon a snag hidden in the river and stopped dead.

The *Mechanic* halted so suddenly, in fact, that people were tumbled from their berths. Clutching their cloaks around themselves, everybody rushed out on deck to find out what had happened. Steamboat accidents were too frequent—and often too dreadful—ever to be taken lightly. At first there was the halfhearted suggestion that it was only a sand bar which had so summarily stopped the *Mechanic*, but when water began rising on the lower deck, they knew a snag must indeed have torn a gash in the wooden hull. And the boat was doomed!

Shaking with alarm, Bastien hastened to waken and dress his master, who was still peacefully slumbering. The captain rushed to get his most important passenger safely ashore, but the general was not to be hurried. He refused at first to leave at all until the women and children had been taken off, but was finally urged toward a small boat. Then he pulled away again and tried to go back to his cabin, while the darkly menacing waters of the Ohio swirled around the wreck, and the packet began to tilt dangerously. Lafayette had left a precious snuffbox behind, one decorated with George Washington's portrait, and he could not bear to consign it to the river. Only when Levasseur insisted did he let his secretary go back for it.

The time was long past midnight, and the river was black as only a river can be on a rainy night. The oars splashed, catching snags, but proceeded safely to the Kentucky shore. The precious passenger and a little girl were helped up the muddy bank first of all. It was then that Lafayette suddenly realized that he had seen nothing of his son. Georges was not with him! The faithful Levasseur hurried back to the steamboat wreck, to see what he could do to help those still aboard and to hunt for Georges Lafayette, while the frantic father called through the rain, over and over—

"Georges . . . Georges . . . where are you?"

The steamboat, lying warped and lopsided in the water, was settling to its grave. Aboard, Levasseur found Bastien hanging desperately to the tilting cabin. They searched hastily and called for Georges, and were about to give up and save themselves when they found him at last, where he was assisting in getting the firemen and engineer off the sinking boat.

Belongings and debris from the wreck began floating free as the *Mechanic* sank lower. Governor Carroll, his trousers rolled up and shoes and stockings off, waded out as far as he dared in the firelit dark and rain to pull in things that were drifting past, among them a mattress. He dragged this soggily to shore and laid it out, with a dry blanket over it. Whereupon, he insisted that the Marquis de Lafayette should lie down and rest. A bonfire made blessed warmth and light. The great French hero and the fifty people in his weary party, hoping for a passing boat that would relieve them before morning, tried to compose themselves in the rain.

But the night was singularly empty of boats. Not many traveled in the dark. The *Mechanic's* captain had only been trying to make up time and get the general to Louisville on schedule, or he would not have ordered the pilot to take the risk of sailing ahead. Morning moved grayly into the world of the river, and, in the dim light, some of the men salvaged food from the wrecked boat. They somehow managed to get a breakfast together.

The durable old general felt as lively as ever, wonderfully excited by the adventure and not at all perturbed, though his hosts were both chagrined and alarmed, fearing that this exposure might bring on a desperate illness and might even cause his death. The nation and the whole world would never let them forget it—they had caused a steamboat to be driven carelessly on a snag and wrecked, with the precious Lafayette aboard, so that he had slept ignominiously on a muddy riverbank, in the rain, as a result of the accident. He— a marquis—had breakfasted like an Indian on smoked venison, damp biscuits, and a lifesaving bottle of wine which had, providentially, been rescued by Governor Carroll.

The captain was too worried to eat anything. He could never forgive himself for this terrible thing. He was a shattered man; his career was ruined. Lafayette tried to comfort him, promised that he and his party would write a declaration which would acquit the commander of the *Mechanic* of any blame or negligence. But the captain could only mourn over what he had permitted to happen.

"Never will my fellow citizens pardon me for the peril to which Lafayette has been exposed!"

He was interrupted by a cheer. Not only one but two steamboats were descending the Ohio from Louisville. The *Highland Laddie* and the *Paragon*, on discovering the wreck and the people on the bank, and on discovering, too, who was there with them, vied with each other to be first to pick up the stranded group. The *Paragon* was assigned the task, however, because of greater room available. Getting everyone quickly aboard and into dry clothing, she reversed her course and hurried back to Louisville.

To the relief of everyone, except perhaps the general, the rest of the journey offered no more such excitement. When Lafayette at last sailed for France in September, he was full of enough tales to tell to his grandchildren for the rest of his life. And the account of the Indians in Alabama, the wilderness along the Mississippi, the Indian woman at Kaskaskia, the old soldier and the wonderful steamboat wreck below Louisville on the Ohio, were at the top of them all.

15. Outlaw Country

It was a night of growing wind on the river as the *Delta Queen* steadily navigated the Ox Bow Bends of the Ohio and pushed toward a murky sunset. The hills darkened, and, below them, the river lay black in their shadows, but the last light of sky and sunset shimmered for a long time in the water ahead of the big boat. It was so windy, with a smell of rain and springtime in it, that the stars themselves seemed to blow and move, yet it was only the boat following a winding channel.

The pilothouse was dark. The pilot sat in blackness. In contrast, the river itself still was visible as a paler path through the night. Lights endanger a pilot's excellent night vision. Even the windows of the lounges in the bow of the boat have heavy curtains and canvas is pulled over them at night.

Probing the shores, hunting for buoys and markers, the

pilot occasionally turned on an arc light whose blue-white beam poked a long finger of query, hunting, finding, moving on. The wind blew, and a migrating loon somewhere up in the star-patterned night called and called again, as if it were near its home lake in the north country, almost a thousand miles away.

All that night the *Delta Queen*, on a high stage of water, "came down the river like a freight train," as Bruce Edgington, night watchman, reported the next morning. The river was so high that the Ohio's movable dams were not needed to hold back water, so that the wickets had been laid down in the river and boats could sail over them, a wonderful saving of time, for the locks were unnecessary.

Consequently, the *Delta Queen* was ahead of time, hours ahead of schedule, as she navigated a bright, shining, brimming, beautiful Ohio River, on a lovely April Monday. She needed to arrive at certain mail pickup and passenger-boarding points at approximately the times announced. She had to find a way to slow down and delay her wonderful progress so that she would reach Paducah at the appointed hour, in the early afternoon.

A towboat pilot would have been delighted to be so speedy. His goal is to get to his destination as fast as possible. This is usually an oil refinery or coal loading dock, where he gets his barges filled and then hurries back up the river to his unloading point, also as fast as possible. But the *Delta Queen*, speedy in spite of herself, had no need to hurry and, in fact, downright refused to be rushed by the impatient river.

A stop at the pirates' cave, Cave-in-Rock, along the southern shore of Illinois, would provide a bonus to the passengers —an unscheduled stop is always a special delight—and would slow down the *Queen's* pace.

Long ago, boats tried to get past this place without the ever-present lookouts on the cliff or at the mouth of the cave discovering them. This was the most dangerous spot on the river: the place where more flatboats and keelboats stopped— and were never heard from again.

The dark mouth of the cave came into focus behind the sycamores as the steamboat turned in a graceful half circle so that her prow was heading into the bank. The big steel landing stage was operated. The mechanism and the electric capstan groaned, and the long stage swung out. But it somehow would not fit properly upon the jagged rocks. It was brought back to its original position, pointing out ahead.

The mate on the lower deck and the captain on the texas did a good deal of ordering about, urging the deck hands to move faster before the *Queen* drifted off, get a head line around a sycamore and a stern line to an elm that was full of silky seeds.

The men ran out the smaller landing stage, directing it from the side of the lower deck out to the rocks. There they built a foundation so that the stage would be steady. They tested everything carefully, so that none of the passengers would trip, turn an ankle or otherwise be discomforted.

The cliffs loomed above, and a trail climbed steeply to the top, where redbud trees were a blur of pink flowers and the first violets of the season blossomed along the path. The cave itself lay upstream a little way from the landing. The breath of spring filled the pleasant sunshine, birds sang, and gulls above the river flashed white wings against a blue sky.

But the cave itself was blank and quiet, its mouth open to the sunshine, its depths forever dark. Not the river itself, but more ancient waters which preceded it, ate out this cavern in the limestone. The mouth of the cave is fifty-five feet wide across the base and extends back 160 feet, with a general width of forty feet, narrowing to the back. This slopes upward in the darkness at the rear to a smaller cavern, into which a sinkhole from above admits light, air, dead leaves, rain and

fresh additions to the heap of earth and debris which has accumulated there in the past centuries.

On either side of the cave's entrance the floor is uneven, arranged in two levels like a stage platform. From outside, the entrance appears as a large, dark arch, inscrutable in the secrets it may hold beyond the rim of sunshine, back in the cool, mysterious darkness.

It was like that long ago, in the days of the pirates. Before then, early men along the river also may have known about the cavern and, on occasion, used its convenient shelter.

This may not always have been possible, for, even now, in time of flood, the river comes into the cave. During the days following the last glacier, the rivers throughout this great drainage area were so much higher than they normally are today, that the cave may often have been filled to the ceiling. Much more recently, during high water, people in boats have entered the cave and have written their names on the otherwise inaccessible ceiling, much to the puzzlement of those who come when the river lies far below the cave. It was only when the river permitted, then, that early hunters no doubt camped here, and their smokes darkened the furrowed roof.

There are Hopewellian Indian mounds on the hill just above the cave itself, as well as on nearby hills. One mound was built on a white sandy-clay floor, laid down on purpose by the builders of the structure more than a thousand years ago. Fourteen bodies were buried on this lowest level, placed on the smooth clay floor itself. Then the mound was built up about three feet, the burials well covered, the earth leveled, and twenty more burials were made, arranged in a circle, in groups of two, three or four individuals, perhaps as families who were laid low by disease.

In the mound were artifacts of great beauty and interest— a dish made of a turtle's shell, complete with a clamshell spoon to serve the corn which no doubt had been buried in the dish; a platform pipe made of ruddy Ohio pipestone, with a falcon effigy as the bowl; and polished spear points and amulets. Many pieces of broken pottery, beads and a shell from the Gulf of Mexico were discovered as evidences of a vanished people.

Who were they? For a long time no one knew. Even now, little is known in detail because they made no written records, only the mute tales told by the things they left behind. But we know that they were rivermen, perhaps the first to navigate the Ohio.

The lives of the Hopewellians centered around the rivers, were inseparable from them. Their mounds and remains are found along the Ohio, the Mississippi, and some of the larger tributaries of both, but seldom far from the watercourses. These people may have come up from the south by way of the rivers, paddling in long dugout cottonwood canoes to find a new village site. Perhaps from some forgotten ancestral link with the cultures of Mexico, they had developed a high form of art in their stonework and clay effigies.

The Hopewellians had a complicated religion and they had knowledge of agriculture. They had settled villages in which people lived in houses made of wood, thatched with reeds or cattail leaves. And it was part of the religious observances that the dead should be buried in mounds high above the rivers. Sometimes temples were also built on mounds especially constructed for them, and some mounds were strange, elaborate symbolisms, such as serpents or turtles or bears, whose meanings no one has fathomed.

The Hopewellians built strong canoes which took them on long journeys into the river wilderness, for these were traders, expert traders who became rich at the business. They took trade goods to barter with other tribes far off, almost as far as the Rocky Mountains, and to the Great Smokies, and to the Gulf of Mexico and Lake Michigan. The Hopewellians were rivermen indeed, but they were conquered by others, the Middle Mississippians, a jealous, predatory people who came upriver in war canoes to destroy the Hopewellians and their way of life. But they could not destroy the cave, and when at last the Mississippians went away, the cave remained, its somber, dark mouth refusing to reveal the secrets of the people who once lived here.

White men, if they knew of the cave, made no mention of it until a certain Monsieur de Lery, a French explorer, came down the wild and unknown Ohio in the early eighteenth century. As he traveled, he made a map of the river and marked the places he discovered. And it was on de Lery's map, for the first time, that there was indicated a *"Caverne dans le Roc."*

A flatboat halted there in 1766. After that, it became a regular stopping point in the unfriendly wilderness, a convenient shelter in time of storm and cold, a wonderful haven for the night, a respite from the long hours on the river. In fact, sometimes a pioneer party divided, leaving some behind to camp at the cave while the others went ahead to secure land. In 1805, four young Kentucky women and their children were discovered living there, comfortable and happy with their spinning wheels and cooking pots and featherbeds, secure in the knowledge that their husbands would return for them in the spring, after getting homesteads ready in the West.

But when the pirates took over the cave, all such pleasant camping projects ceased. The cave became a place of horror. It was an obstruction on the river, hindering peaceful craft from proceeding down to the Mississippi and New Orleans.

For some time, there was only a dark mystery as to just what was happening to so many boats and men who were never heard from again after they set off down the Ohio. In fact, matters grew so desperate that no tidings could rightly be expected of any boat after it had passed the fatal Cave-in-Rock, unless it was extremely fortunate or extremely well armed, or had nothing of value aboard. Even when the trouble was finally pinpointed to this spot, it took some time before frontier justice stepped in and routed the marauders out to their punishment.

It seems that a certain reputable Samuel Mason, who had fought in the American Revolution and who was known heretofore as a law-abiding man of education and some breeding, became a very different person when the war was over. The unruly wildness of the frontier infected him with its power, and he turned outlaw.

In 1797, he had taken over Cave-in-Rock, had changed his name to Wilson, had put up a large, prominent sign outside the cave, visible to downbound boats (there was little or no upbound traffic before steamboats) and waited for the customers, the victims and the loot.

The sign read:

WILSON'S LIQUOR VAULT AND HOUSE FOR ENTERTAINMENT

The cave was well stocked with stolen supplies of food and liquor, and provided beds for the weary travelers, though not all were permitted to sleep in them. At the start, Wilson (or Mason) let the cave's hospitality become known along the river. He established the kindly reputation of the "house for entertainment," and many boats got into the habit of making it a regular stop. The sign was an irresistible lure to men weary of the river and their own much diminished stock of Old Monongahela or homemade applejack.

After a bit, boats stopping at the cave were not heard from again. Men dropped out of sight and never returned home. Cargoes of produce and other goods, bound for the markets of Natchez and New Orleans, did not reach their goals nor did their owners come back with money from the transactions.

As each boat stopped at the cave, those aboard were given two choices—join the gang or be set adrift in a small boat, with the freedom to escape. A number of the rougher element, including thieves and gamblers looking for fertile fields, chose to stay. Others, in alarm, chose to depart in the questionable safety of a small boat.

But Samuel Mason-Wilson wasn't really giving anyone a choice. He had about forty-five confederates camped down on Hurricane Island, below the cave, to take care of the objectors, and there were more bandits in the woods around the cave, in case anyone tried to make a break for it on foot.

Thus, when the released and thankful prisoners were set adrift in a skiff and the craft invariably floated with the current and lodged against the sand bars of Hurricane Island, the victims were dispatched by the thugs waiting there. The bodies were disposed of neatly in the inscrutable river. Mason did things up well. He left no loose ends, no blood to be accounted for, not even any stray bodies to be explained. He also assured himself that there would be no terrified travelers rushing back to civilization with tales of how they had been treated at the famed HOUSE FOR ENTERTAINMENT.

But when Mason's gang was joined by ferocious Micajah and Wiley Harpe and their women, things changed for the worse—if that was possible, and it was. Mason robbed and killed for money. He didn't torture people. His murders were quick and to the point. But the Harpes killed because they enjoyed a good, leisurely, bloody slaughter, and they knew how to put on the fine touches to make it the ultimate in horror, both for those who were victims and for those who came upon the remains afterward. Even their fellow bandits and murderers, with whom the Harpes occasionally consorted, were disgusted and repelled by the sadistic killers and the way in which they delighted in murdering little children and women, as well as men.

Robbing never seemed of much moment to the hateful Harpes. They were wanderers, killing as they went. When things grew too hot for them, Big Harpe and Little Harpe moved on, leaving behind them a path of blood as they rode up the Wilderness Road or the Natchez Trace. Since both of these trails led indirectly by side paths to Ford's Ferry, crossing the Ohio not far from Cave-in-Rock, it was inevitable that they should come at last to the cave and stay a while.

But, after committing atrocities on people whom Samuel Mason had no especial wish to molest, the Harpes left suddenly, with irate pioneers on their trail again. Big Harpe was finally caught and killed. Much later, Little Harpe was tracked down and met the same fate along the Natchez Trace. Sam Mason who, by that time, had left the cave because it was becoming too well known by the law-abiding, also spent some time preying on the well-enriched homeward bound travelers on the Trace. And that was where Mason, too, pirate of Cave-in-Rock, met his end.

With the departure of bandits and pirates, the cave along the Ohio lay empty and innocent, with the sunshine at its mouth, but the terrible spirits of the murderous Harpes still somehow lingered, and the depredations of Samuel Mason could not be forgotten. The sign was washed away in a flood, and the cave finally lay purged of evil, scrubbed out by high water and broomed out by the wind. Even so, few boats stopped there any more. With the coming of steamboats in the first quarter of the nineteenth century, travelers were able to move right on down the river without the need for pausing at doubtful points for rest and refreshment. As the flatboats and keelboats grew fewer, so did overnight visitors to the cave.

Some years later, it became the headquarters of a band of counterfeiters who were very quiet about what they were up to. They had no wish to attract attention to themselves by hailing passing boats. Occasionally, a steamer going by at night would see a light at the cave and dark figures silhouetted against it, and someone would tell once again the stories of Big Harpe and Little Harpe and Mason's HOUSE FOR ENTERTAINMENT.

When the counterfeiters went away, the cave again was empty except for the chipmunks which denned up there for the winter. The sycamores outside grew bigger and always, in the spring, the scarlet and golden flowers of wild columbine hung their bells around the rocks and along the trail to the cave. A village named Cave-in-Rock sprang up in the hollow nearby, and in 1909 the cave and the area on the heights above it were made into an Illinois state park.

It was here that Walt Disney, a few years ago, brought

cast, directors and crew to film *Davy Crockett and the River Pirates* in the authentic setting of Cave-in-Rock, but after this brief prominence and excitement, the village again settled down to its placid existence by the river.

No more Hopewellians, no more Indians, no more pirates, no more excitement—yet their shadows still haunt the cave, still flit among the sycamores and cedars on the cliffs, somehow bringing to the people of the *Delta Queen* a little of the flavor of the past, all wrapped in bird song and garnished with violets.

It was an innocent cave now, quiet and voiceless beside the glittering Ohio. And then the big bell called, and the river called, and we came back from our explorations, picking our way over the stones, until everyone was aboard.

As the boat backed away from her impromptu landing and circled into the broad river, the paddle wheel churning white water and kicking wind-tossed spray, at last heading downstream, I stood by the railing and watched the dark mouth of the cave vanish behind the trees. And while I watched, I held something in my hand. . . . I had found a flint arrowhead among the rocks near the cave . . . an arrowhead lost how many hundreds or thousands of years ago, by what man, for what reason . . . in that wild land of rivers and caves and hills aglint with spring?

16. Futile Fort along the River

The *Delta Queen* made her stop at Paducah, Kentucky, at the mouth of the Tennessee River. The passengers who went ashore soon straggled warmly back to the boat and relaxed in the shade with cold drinks, to watch the activity in the shipyard, or to observe a mass baptism which was taking place along the shore, not far from the *Delta Queen*. We were all relieved when the boat set off again and stirred up a little breeze in the humid river atmosphere which was replacing the chilliness we had left behind at Cincinnati and in the windy Ox Bow Bends.

The starboard side of the boat was shady and it was here that dozens of passengers sat in deck chairs while the low green shores of Illinois went past. Some people were immersed in books; others dozed; the rest were intent on the landscape, on the river, on the passing towboats. In comfortable relaxation, we could sit and watch the scenery go by in an unending procession of change, while the paddle wheel sturdily churned up the river behind us, and the wind whipped the many-starred Union Jack on the jack staff high above the bow.

The big chimneys of the atomic power plant at Joppa momentarily patterned the sky . . . and were past. Then, a little way downstream, three sturdy poles from which fluttered three very different flags came into view.

I made out the figure of a man in front of the poles, a man of bronze leaning gracefully against a pillar, as if against a tree trunk in the forest, surveying the river, the sky, and the far Kentucky shore. George Rogers Clark was still guarding the remains of old Fort Massac, watching over the welfare of the river and the Northwest Territory for which he had fought. Behind him waved the flags of the United States, France and Great Britain. At various times, each one had claimed rights to this spot, but the river itself had claimed it longest and most of all.

Massac was a fort which never amounted to much of anything. It was never really attacked. Hardly anyone liked it or coveted it, and garrisons had no wish to be stationed there. From the fort, as Clark from his pedestal of glory was still seeing it, the Ohio River lay glimmering and misty, within view for twenty-four miles up and down, as Indian, French, British and American eyes also must have seen it.

The fort commanded an excellent view of the vital river route and the distant shore. But there was no clear look to the rear, none back there where the riverbank forests, heavy and almost jungle-like with big pecan trees, sycamores and cypresses, tangled with wild grapevines and matted with nettles and wild cucumber, had stretched away into the vast, mysterious swamps of southern Illinois.

So, in spite of a situation which commanded the Ohio River

so well that no boat could creep up undetected to the sturdy log walls of the fort, the French were always uneasy. There was a persistent, if unproved, story of what had happened here long before, when the fort was first built. French soldiers, it was said, bored with inactivity, gazing in vacant *ennui* at the far shore, suddenly woke up. A great many large black bears were down on the Kentucky bank. The garrison came to life, delighted with the prospect of some excitement at last. A bear hunt! Anything for some fun, something to break the monotony of life in this forsaken post.

So, leaving half of the force in command, the other half went by boat across the river, to stalk and shoot the "bears." These, however, were not authentic bruins, but Indians dressed in bearskins, who promptly and gleefully ambushed the eager French. At the same time, a number of Shawnees who were waiting, hidden behind the pecan trees back of the fort itself, descended upon it and killed most of the men who remained behind, that is, all those who had eagerly gathered on the shore to watch the bear hunt from a distance.

Later on, however, no one could be really sure whether this was a true story or something told as a joke to frighten the next garrison. Nevertheless, it kept later garrisons always a bit uneasy and afraid of being taken in by guile. They spent a somewhat miserable, nervously alert, mosquito-bitten, boring vigil in a place where nothing much ever seemed to happen, and where the summers were uncomfortably hot and humid, the winters cold and windy.

The French held Fort Massac for seven years (1757–1764). There was no Indian trouble, no attacks of any kind to make the long days more interesting or the summer's humidity more bearable. The Shawnees and Miamis disobligingly let Fort Massac quite alone after that perhaps mythical bear episode. When the Treaty of Paris ceded the Illinois territory to the British, the French soldiers no doubt packed their belongings thankfully and departed to more lively and rewarding posts.

And the stout cypress and oak logs which made up the sturdy fort on the Ohio River shore, with forests and swamps at its back and the unpredictable river at its doorstep, fell into decay. When a roving band of Cherokees discovered that it was empty, they did a thorough job of wrecking what remained—too late, however, to lend any glory or excitement to the departed French. The forest again moved into the cleared land, as forests do when they are given half a chance, particularly along the river. The remains of the fort crumbled or were taken off by high waters and the wild creatures came back.

But during the American Revolution, repercussions of the war and its issues were felt far away along the Ohio and the Mississippi. Americans who sympathized with the Colonial cause did their part to further the conflict by conveying powder, purchased from the French and Spanish in New Orleans, by keelboat up the Mississippi and Ohio Rivers to Virginia, where it was carried overland to the battlegrounds. More and more, the western rivers were recognized as the base of attack on the British to the north, as well as a link with the French and Spanish sympathizers.

In 1778, George Rogers Clark, with 175 men, came down the Ohio in canoes from Virginia, and they landed where old Fort Massac lay in ruins. From here, they started northwest on the old trail through the cypress swamps to the French town of Kaskaskia, northwesterly on the banks of the Mississippi. With little ado and with quick, razor-sharp drama, on the Fourth of July, 1778, Clark captured British-held Kaskaskia for the Americans. The following late winter, he and his men marched through a flooded Illinois country, over much of the trail, submerged at that season, which the buffalo had taken between the Mississippi and the Wabash.

He surprised General Hamilton at Vincennes, and he took this British-held city on the Wabash for America.

Fort Massac was rebuilt in 1794, when President George Washington, disturbed by trouble with Spain, sent out Mad Anthony Wayne to refortify that strategic spot along the Ohio. Captain Zebulon Pike was in command. His son, who bore the same illustrious name, was subaltern—a son who, one day, after a long and heartbreaking journey across the western plains, would discover a mountain to be named in his honor. Before that, too, he would head an expedition up from St. Louis by keelboat, on the Upper Mississippi, hunting for the elusive headwaters of the river. Many a man left his mark on the rivers, over and over again, in strange and complicated patterns.

For a time, the Spanish Conspiracy threatened to place Kentucky and nearby parts of the United States once more under Spanish rule. A thousand men were now stationed at Cantonment Wilkinson-Ville, a few miles down the Ohio from Massac. Men at the fort were alerted twenty-four hours a day. Every rustling in the forest, every splashing in the cypress swamp, every big carp that leaped out of the Ohio and fell back noisily, might have heralded the capture of the fort. But the attack never came, the Spanish Conspiracy never materialized; and finally, after a later period of alertness during the War of 1812, the fort was abandoned.

It had never been really important as an army post. It had never really defended anything against anyone. It was always the fort which no one ever attacked, the post in which men yawned and slapped mosquitoes for want of excitement, the place which was always about to be surrounded by an enemy who never came. The insects and rattlesnakes in the swamps and river shores were probably its greatest menace. As late as 1929–30, when a road was finally put through the

big cypress swamp near the fort, road crews killed stout-
bodied rattlers six feet long, and the mosquitoes were as bad
as ever.

The fort vanished, but the view and the memories and the
river remain. In 1908, Fort Massac State Park, near Metropo-
lis, Illinois, and near the highway bridge to Paducah, Kentucky, was dedicated for the use of the people. The outline
of the fort was marked with logs, but a full restoration has
never been accomplished. Like the fort itself, the restoration
is slow and nothing much ever happens to its progress. Three
large, tree-sized flagpoles fly the flags of France, England and
America, and Clark is there, giving life and meaning to the
place.

He is the irresistible reminder of past excitement along
the river—he, the explorer and conqueror, dynamic George
Rogers Clark; the adventurer, the dreamer, the man who
loved the rivers and the West, follower of the distant horizon
and the far blue sky. He rests casually there, with his eyes
looking ever outward and focused far away.

17. Today's River

Visible or invisible, the past is always present on the river. Pirates and bandits; Clark and his men; the ghosts of steamboats; the unmarked sites of wrecks and explosions; the long-gone landings where steamboats lined up for half a mile or more; the splendor of the passing packets. It is easy to feel, aboard the *Delta Queen*, modern though she may be, that the past is more important than today on the river.

But today's Ohio is a vital stream of commerce. It begins where the Allegheny and the Monongahela join at Pittsburgh to form the Ohio River, which flows 981 miles to the spot where it merges in the Mississippi, at the southern tip of Illinois. And this Ohio River is alive, more important and far busier than it has been at any time in its history, for it is an atomic energy lifeline which is as up-to-date as today and as vital as tomorrow. Upon these waters travel hundreds of modern boats, hauling millions of tons of potential power—coal from the mines at Yankeetown and Huntington and the Green River in Kentucky.

Coal is the fuel powering atomic energy production at Portsmouth, Ohio, and its auxiliary power plants situated down the river, as well as at the five great power plants of the American Gas and Electric System. Tremendous chimneys, silhouetted like big harps against the sky, and huge functional structures mark from a distance one of these mighty operations.

To them, day and night, come the endless loads of coal carried in great steel barges pushed by towboats. The *Delta Queen* had passed many of these boats—the *Philip Sporn*, the *Raymond A. Salvati*, the *Patsy Hillman*, the *La Salle*, the *Gene Hutchinson*, the *Peace*, the *Cypress*, the *Coal King*, the *Eleanor Gordon*, the *Coal City*, the *Aliquippa*—the big boats and the small, pushing tightly integrated barges in vast tows, carrying great compacted heaps of glossy coal, potential power for the nation.

They and those other white towboats pushing oil barges, or motorcars, or sulphur, or bauxite, or crushed rock, or molasses, or chemicals, or steel, formed a scattered procession upon the waterway. There was seldom a very long stretch of time or river without one of them in sight. This was no empty stream, no former highway, now deserted by boats because the Steamboat Era had gone—with only one exception, the *Queen*.

She wasn't the only steam-powered boat operating, either. There were still steam towboats operating—the big *Tenaru River*, the *Ohio*, the *Guadalcanal*—putting black smoke on the sky. But most of the craft were Diesel boats, sleek and white, for no new steamboats have been built since 1942. The Diesel engines are enclosed in neat white cabinets; and, instead of stern wheel or side wheel, these efficient, powerful vessels are driven by screw propellers, many of the newer models enclosed in a large, tubular structure called a Kort nozzle, which gives greater power and thrust to propellers and rudders.

The towboats are as comfortable inside as a hotel; most are air-conditioned, have excellent food, comfortable lounges and bedrooms. They are clean-lined, streamlined, beautiful. But they are not for passengers. They are only for the hand-picked crews of often well-educated young men who man these boats. Sometimes the tow of barges is so large in one massing of cargo that the boat pushing the load looks like an ant shoving a loaf of bread.

The towboats make of the Ohio a lively liquid avenue, yet it still has wide gaps of forest and swamp along its shores. Much of this shows little-diminished wilderness. There are still the tall, brooding hills covered with oaks whose aroma, at night, comes to the passing boat as distinctly as the smell of the bottomland weed field. But the upper Ohio, down from the port of Pittsburgh itself, contains an almost con-tinuous line-up of towns, business and river-born industry.

World ports, shipbuilders, steel mills, bridge construction firms, manufacturers of material for skyscrapers—steel for the Empire State Building came from the American Bridge Com-pany—all these are located along the Ohio, as are glass com-panies, aluminum and chemical corporations, pottery makers, builders and repairers of towboats . . . and always the pro-ducers of power, power, power, lifeblood of the Ohio.

To provide it, towboats must continue to come with their cargoes of coal, in barges carrying a thousand tons each. In four days' time, an Ohio River power plant will use 33,000 tons of coal, poured into the nation's greatest atomic energy project.

The Ohio has been busy since the end of World War II, and so has the once slumbering Mississippi. And now, as the

development of the St. Lawrence Seaway continues, the inland rivers are connected directly with the Atlantic Ocean
and the ports of the world. Great as today is for the river,
tomorrow will be greater.

And to be prosperous, to do the job demanded of it, the
river must be navigable. That was always the problem in the
past, when the whims of the river were uncontrollable by
man, and he and his steamboats and rafts and keelboats had to
wait for enough water to float them, or had to wallow in an
excess of it when floods ravaged the valley.

The U.S. Corps of Engineers built a series of levees and
they built a lot of locks and dams. They dredged a channel
nine feet deep. They turned the Ohio into a controlled canal,
put high walls along the river towns and deep water where
it used to be shallow. They built movable dams which could
be raised or lowered to suit the water level. They could hold
back the water in deep pools for navigation, yet could be laid
down on the river bottom in high water, when dams were
unnecessary. By the middle of the twentieth century, however, the bear-trap wicket dams and the narrow locks were
outmoded, obsolete bottlenecks which were holding back
the smooth flow of traffic.

The river had to be remodeled again. The fifty-three short
and narrow locks and the fifty-three small, awkward dams
had to be changed.

Today, one new, big, immovable dam and a lock chamber
110 feet wide and 1,200 feet long (the old ones were only
half that size) replaces as many as five of the old locks and
dams. There is a smaller auxiliary chamber for shorter tows
and small boats. It sometimes took hours for a large tow to
be broken apart, locked through piecemeal, and fastened together again on the other side. Now they do it in eight
minutes.

Passing and being passed by many a modern towboat, the

Delta Queen was a link between yesterday and today. She was moving along a river in which and beside which the past and present were inseparable, like steamboat and towboat, each with a job to do.

And just as the great coal piles and tall chimneys of the power plants were a reality of today, so was yesterday still vivid and real. We were following where flatboat and keelboat once traveled, bearing upon their decks the eager searchers for far shores and new truths.

Last night, we had passed two points on the river: Rockport, Indiana, perched in elderly serenity on a cliff, and the raw clay cut which was the mouth of the Wabash. Both had a large importance long ago which is hardly visible today.

It was below that Indiana cliff that young Abraham Lincoln, in 1828, built his first flatboat, and from this point he set off on his first journey. To the boys and young men of long-gone yesterdays, the flatboat was the symbol of freedom and adventure, the emblem of escape. And Abraham Lincoln, aged seventeen, was impatient with the conditions at home, tired of working himself half to death for thirty-seven cents a day in James Taylor's cornfields and running Taylor's ferry besides. He was tired of watching steamboats always going past the bottomland field where he was plowing and not stopping, ever, to take him along. He was ready for escape, ripe for action, eager for change. And the chance came when the father of his friend, Allen Gentry, felt unequal to making the annual trip by flatboat with produce for the markets of New Orleans.

Allen would go, and he hoped Abraham Lincoln would accompany him as crew, so they could make the trip together.

This was the doorway to adventure for young Abraham, just as it was for many another boy who lived along the river and yearned to follow its course. The big flatboat was eighteen feet wide and eighty feet long, roofed over to protect the barrels of flour, salt, cornmeal and salt pork, the lard, whiskey, apples and maple sugar. It was guided by a long hickory sweep or steering oar. The river took the craft at the current's own pace, at the water's whims—usually at about four miles an hour. To any young fellow whose fastest speed hitherto had been behind a plow, this was glorious. The unpredictable Mississippi was a great adventure, too, and New Orleans was a different world. As for the ride back on a real steamboat, that was the climax to the best to be had in life. The river opened to the boy a whole new concept of people and their different ways of living, in fact, of the world.

And just as the memory of Lincoln was vivid along the Ohio, so also was a strange craft which had come down from Pittsburgh in 1825 and headed up into the mouth of the Wabash. The ghost of the Boatload of Knowledge, seeker after a better way of life, is still on the rivers. A remodeled keelboat, it was loaded with books, a piano, musical instruments, artists, writers, scientists, teachers and pupils for the noble experiment of Robert Owen's New Harmony community. The boat had started from Pittsburgh in early winter, bound for Indiana. The original plan had been to go by steamboat—it would have been a fast trip on a craft like that. But the river was too low, so a keelboat was remodeled to suit the people of this experiment in living. The keelboat would get them to New Harmony, more slowly than a steamboat, of course, but surely. However, the craft was caught in a sudden freeze and was immobilized for weeks in the thick ice along the Pennsylvania shores.

But eventually, the undaunted people on the Boatload of Knowledge, who had made good use of piano and books and collecting equipment during their enforced layover, were on their way, once more. They arrived at the doorstep of New Harmony in a snowstorm.

The community, based on the principles of brotherly love, harmony, education and the division of wealth, work and wisdom, did not survive for very long. Its ideals did not fit the pattern of human independence with its unaccountable foibles. The community dispersed, but New Harmony remained as a river town. Some of the houses built by those people who rode down the Ohio in the wonderful Boatload of Knowledge during a cold December still stand, monuments to some of the experiments in human relations which had their origin along the rivers.

By nine o'clock on Monday night, the *Delta Queen* was passing Cairo, the last city on the Ohio before it empties into the Mississippi. At this triangular tip of Illinois, the two rivers merge as one enormous stream.

Cairo never attained the importance for which it seemed to be intended. Located on a neck of land bounded on one side by the Mississippi and on the other by the Ohio, Cairo could have become a city like Pittsburgh, commanding two great rivers, but somehow it never did.

For a long time after it was planned on paper by Kaskaskia bankers, Cairo remained only a swamp. It became a wooding stop for steamboats, but still was a quagmire, beset with snakes and mosquitoes. When at last, in 1818, a town began to grow, there was always trouble with high water, soggy ground and the malaria brought on by mosquitoes.

Not until Cairo became General Grant's headquarters during the War Between the States did the city really develop. Here was based the northern fleet of gunboats, the armorclads, the rams and other fighting vessels which waited impatiently to get down the river. Only the great chain across the Mississippi at Columbus, Kentucky, kept them from moving southward into the fray.

Before the war, Cairo had been a southern city which, by an accident of nature, had been placed on the north side of the Ohio. In almost all of its interests and inclinations, it was more southern than northern—in the soft way of speech of its inhabitants, in the great fragrant white magnolia blossoms on tall trees along the streets, in the mimosas and crepe myrtles in its gardens, in the snowy bolls of cotton in the bottom-land fields. The hot, humid climate, the short winter, the way of life, all were southern. But the War Between the States demanded that it be northern. From this strategic point, General Grant pursued the war down the river, to open its length for Federal boats.

After the war, steamboats lined up for a great distance along the Cairo waterfront, on the Ohio side. This was the city's most prosperous time. But when the *Delta Queen* passed by at night, on an April evening, there were no boats at all to be seen. And the great concrete and stone levee and sea wall rose defiantly, like a dark fortress, above a river which lay far below and which seemed to possess no likelihood of ever being a menace.

But Cairo knows that river, knows that it has its measure. The sixty-five-foot sea wall with its gateways which can be closed against the rising water, is surely tall enough. Cairo has never been really flooded, but it has come so close to it that high water is never taken lightly by this city caught in a levee-walled lowland between two of the greatest rivers in America.

That night, while the evening dance and music proceeded gaily in the boat's dining room, the *Delta Queen* headed under the three green lights of the railroad bridge, passed beneath the highway bridge joining Cairo with Kentucky, joining North with South in a friendly handclasp. She turned and soon was rapidly leaving the city lights behind.

Under her now was dark Mississippi River water—water stretching tremendously in all directions, while boat lights, channel marker lights and city lights were all mirrored in profound beauty under a lowering sky and a rainy wind. The *Delta Queen* had left the busy, storied, historic, several worlds of the Ohio and was moving swiftly on the high, muddy Mississippi.

18. River Wilderness

Moving downstream by day on this first voyage of the year, we had seen spring grow visibly on the river's banks. Cottonwoods and willows had been bare when the steamboat paddled past the Ohio River shores, but by the time she reached the Mississippi, they were green with new leaves. We passed close enough to the banks for the songs of migrant birds to come into the staterooms where we slept, to wake us gently. White egrets picked their way along the driftwood at the water's edge, and sand bars jutted out, crowned with young, greening willows. Masses of golden flowers, the early groundsel, carpeting the river woods, made a yellow border along the sheer top of the riverbank—gold for miles.

The water was high and rising higher. The full extent of the sand bars could only be guessed at—the pilots gave them a wide berth. Many were completely submerged, while the great bulk of others was hidden, with only a deceptively small portion still showing above the surging, muddy surface. Like an iceberg, a sand bar is two-thirds hidden. And it is the hidden part of which the boats must beware.

In the flat Tennessee bottomlands, men with mules or tractors were plowing fields for cotton. There were unpainted shacks up on short stilts in these fields, other houses at ground level farther back. Each had a rounded, ostrichlike, china-berry tree or two beside the open, unscreened front door. These chinaberries are a fixture beside the shacks in the cotton country. The trees make a cool shade in summer. In winter, the numerous branches are trimmed off for firewood. Each spring, a new crop of twigs springs forth to provide for the next winter's kindling. The flowers, in great yellow-green clusters, attract bees, which, in turn, may live in a hive behind the house. The chinaberry is the lazy man's tree in the South.

The river that day was very muddy, the color and thickness of chocolate-milk, unbelievably turgid with the earth of half a continent. Many passengers aboard, coming from the clear-water country of Washington and Oregon, or Maine and New York, had never seen such murky liquid, such incal-culably muddy fluid. Nor had they ever seen such an endless wilderness of trees, stretching from river to horizon, as far as they could make out.

Those people from the West had felt that they knew the wilderness; it belonged in that wild country of the Sierras and the Cascades. But here, from the deck of a river boat, all they could see for miles was trees . . . willows of varying sizes on the banks, higher land covered with oaks and maples, cypresses in the swamps. The *Delta Queen* might paddle rapidly along for half a day without passing even a fisher-man, and no towns at all. We were observing the scenery of the river very much as early travelers had seen it, for the river bottoms have changed very little.

It is such unstable country, completely at the command of the river, that towns are unsafe if they are too close by. Those which did have the temerity to be built near the river have long since been swept away or eaten up by a change in the channel. To give the Mississippi enough room to writhe in its sinuous course to the sea, man long since has learned to let it have the bottomlands. Towns are on the bluffs, out of reach of the river, or several miles away, beyond the series of levee embankments which control the Mississippi on its rampages.

So it was through a wilderness of trees below a sky piled high with massive white clouds that the *Delta Queen* moved, her paddle wheel churning the mud to creamy foam and sending up in a flurry of flight some of the flocks of cormorants, coots and migrant ducks swimming ahead of us.

The strong wind was making the sand bars smoke. Baked and dry, like pale cornmeal shining in the spring sunshine, they were being lifted up by the beating wind. The dry substance was cast like smoke into the air, hurled aloft in funnels and whirls, or blurred like fog across the river at a distance. It punished the passing vessel with a sandblasting of fine grit which got into eyes and stung faces.

The sheer banks of the east shore were being picked up by a violent wind which seemed to rush straight along the water, then rise in a sudden upward swoop, carrying the sand with it in jets and fountains, like water and spray, throwing it high into the air. For miles the sand banks were fountaining, the sand bars were steaming, and the mudbanks, as they always do, were sending quiet showers and small cascades of earth grains into the gnawing water. Wind and water and gravity were conspiring to endlessly change the face of the river landscape, a grain at a time, a mudbank at a time, a sand bar's surface or a sand bank's substance, so that neither the river nor its shores are ever the same from day to day or from hour to hour.

Far ahead, suddenly, after many miles of forests and sand bars and wind, we saw the afternoon sunshine light the incredible towers and brick buildings of Memphis. After 117 miles of apparently uninhabited country since passing Caruthersville, Missouri, the approach to the opulent city of Memphis, situated on the rise of the Fourth Chickasaw Bluff, was impressive. It was like coming through the days of the early Steamboat Era to meet the modern present in a bath of hot spring sunshine.

Memphis has struggled for years to maintain an open waterfront. The Wolf River, coming from the north into the Mississippi, has contrived, by its outwash of mud, sand and debris, to build up bars and islands which, long ago, might have blocked the waterfront completely. If dredging and pile dikes and other drastic means had not kept the harbor open, Memphis by now might have found itself far from navigable water.

President's Island, on which Andrew Jackson once owned land, is the largest in the Mississippi, covering 32,000 acres in front of Memphis. Mud Island, however, was formed in this century. The Spanish-American War gunboat, *Aphrodite,* waiting for a rise in the river in order to proceed to St. Louis, was moored for eight months in the Memphis harbor. Sand and mud gathered under the hull of the vessel, so that, by the time it had gone on its way, an island of some size and durability had formed. By 1911 this was above water, and it has since continued to grow until it almost blocks the waterfront.

But Memphis keeps a clear channel out to the main part of the river. Into this, rounding Mud Island, the *Delta Queen* headed, and nosed in among small commercial craft to tie up at the store boat, whose landing stage provided a direct connection with the cobbled waterfront.

Memphis has not only struggled valiantly against islands blocking her view, she has also labored to present to the river a beautiful shore, and this has been no easy task. Most river cities have ignored their waterfronts, usually employing them for dumps, debris and makeshift docks for pleasure craft and towboats. Memphis, however, nobly situated on the Chickasaw Bluff, has removed unsightly things from its shore.

Polished, rounded cobblestones hold the bank in place against the endless chewing of the river, while up a distance from the usual limit of high water is the parkway, planted with flowers and grass and set with hawthorn and dogwood trees. Parks are at each end of this area, and, on a spring day, the sight of dozens of dogwoods in full, snowy bloom, blossoming tulips, green grass and leafing trees offers a delightful welcome to the big city, an embellishment to the river.

Confederate Park and Jefferson Davis Park have cannon and benches, pigeons and mockingbirds. The cannon are a sobering reminder of the hatred they represented when the North was sending gunboats down the river to conquer Memphis, and Memphis replied with artillery on the bluff, and with her own gunboats in the harbor. But war and regional enmity are over now. The mockingbirds, on a sunny April day, sing alike for Northerners and Southerners, and the pigeons accept crumbs from any hands presenting them.

Memphians say that this spot is the oldest known to white men along the Mississippi. They say that in 1541 Hernando De Soto stood on this bluff and beheld the great, relentless river which barred his crossing. De Soto Park, with an Indian mound crowning it, and a few more cannon for good measure, marks the spot where he stood—but historians, more literal, suggest that the place was more probably about thirty miles downstream, and has since been washed away by the changing course of the river. In more than four hundred years, the Mississippi has wandered back and forth across its valley and has obliterated old landmarks.

We went ashore and met summer heat. Up along the warehouse district, fluffs of cotton scampered on a hot breeze across the pavement. Outside of seed stores there were tomato plants, buckets of seed peanuts and seed cotton, while along the big streets in the heart of the city, the willow oaks were putting out sparkling leaves of a chartreuse color. It was like summer in Memphis—girls in sleeveless dresses, men without coats, the sun uncomfortably warm.

At the foot of the hill, the chocolate-colored river glittered in the afternoon sunshine. It and the steamboat beckoned, and the fluffs of cotton led the way as the wind veered to the east and blew the white stuff down the cobblestones.

As the sun slid behind the willows on the Arkansas shore, night came over Memphis and the Mississippi, over the quiet *Delta Queen*. Lights began to spark along the waterfront, on vessels anchored there, on the small harbor tugboats, on channel markers farther out, and in the tall buildings of Memphis, giving them greater stature than they had appeared to have in daylight. When, at last, the *Delta Queen's* great bell tolled its warning call, twelve times echoing against the buildings and the dogwood-patterned hill, then tolling nine times more, and the all-ashore call went out, night had come to the river.

The stern wheel churned and the rudders moved as the *Queen* backed out and circled in the narrow harbor while the magnificent array of city lights—of yellow and white and scarlet and green—was patterned against the dark sky and reflected in the shimmering liquid blackness of the water. Heading toward the arch of green lights marking the bridges,

the *Delta Queen* blew her farewell blast and was on her way
again, down the dark and beckoning river.

The next morning was cloudy and cool and windy as the
Delta Queen, in the safety of a high river stage, seeking slack
water, cut close to the banks. Birds sang in the morning light
—titmice and Carolina wrens with a great loudness, white-
throated sparrows on their way to northern woods, warblers
flashing bright gold, mockingbirds trilling, cardinals whistling.
A black vulture, his wings wrapped around him like a rusty
cloak against the chill dampness of dawn, sat on a broken tree
and observed the passing boat. The willows were by now all
green, and a great many were golden with bloom, scattering
color for miles along the Mississippi and casting pollen to
the winds and waters.

The river was a different color, a pale gray-brown. The
chocolate-colored water belonged upstream. Mile by mile, it
was ever-changing—its color, its smell, its shores, its growing
look of spring.

About this time each year, several flights of white pelicans
come up the Mississippi from where they have wintered in
southern Louisiana, and go to Minnesota, the Dakotas, or
Canada to nest. For more than a thousand miles, they follow
the exact course of the river, spending a good deal of time
resting on sand bars and feeding in the waters. April is the
time—April, if one is on a boat which does not pass them at
night, or on the wrong day . . . if. . . .

The *Delta Queen's* morning paper, a mimeographed sheet
which is found at everyone's plate at breakfast, announced,
"this is the day to look for pelicans." No one could be sure,
of course, but so many people aboard were interested in the
wildlife of the river that the announcement would at least
give them added incentive for watching the sand bars and the
sky for a sight of huge white birds with black wing tips.

At half past seven that April morning, when I was taking a turn around the deck, and people in the dining room were reading "this is the day to see pelicans," a mass of white appeared like a snowbank on a distant sand bar. Pelicans, and right on time!

Pelicans, indeed! The purser's office, with the public address system used for announcing special sights and events, was not yet open. But strollers on deck were alerted, and Bruce Edgington, everyone's special courier and friend, hurried to the dining room.

From the doorway, he announced dramatically:

"Pelicans off the starboard bow!"

And the breakfasters, who had just that moment been reading about these fascinating birds, with one accord and with much confusion to the waiters, got up hastily from their bacon and eggs and crowded to the windows.

The *Delta Queen* was just abreast of the birds; Captain

Hampton was running in as close as he dared. We were within a few yards of the sand bar on which more than two hundred large white pelicans, all facing in the same direction, were walking slowly on their yellow feet. Their immense wings with the black tips were folded neatly or, on occasion, raised, so we could see their great size, which becomes a nine-foot spread in flight. We observed the yellow throat pouches, the snowy feathers, the pale eyes. "Those pelicans were so close," one man commented in awe, "you could see the whites of their eyes!"

And then the *Delta Queen* had passed the birds, and the breakfasters went back to their meal. All day, they were considerably set up over what they had seen, and somewhat lorded it over the late-risers who had missed this choice sight. Several scattered pelicans were seen later that day, but nothing as spectacular as the number seen at close range.

Thereafter, the passengers' interest in the wildlife of the Mississippi was much increased, and whenever a flock of ducks, a group of black cormorants perched on snags, a low-coasting eagle, a flight of wood ibises on an updraft, or a snowy egret with bright yellow feet was discovered, a battery of binoculars was brought into play, from the sundeck to the cabin deck.

Again the wilderness, the look of the untouched land, closed in. The *Delta Queen* was navigating a series of sweeping bends, was passing through a series of cutoffs which had shortened the route years ago. Although we are accustomed to saying that the Mississippi is 2,552 miles long, it has been man-shortened by 151 miles, so that the length is actually 2,401 miles. Yet the river is so changeable that even man's meddling may not last long. And while we have shortened it in the middle, it is lengthening itself at the far end, where it goes out into the sea and has formed the delta. Who can say, accurately at least, how long the Mississippi is?

The cutoffs eliminated some of the great sweeping loops which had given the river time to get to where it was going, sliding down the continental slope in a safe and leisurely way, not pushing everything before it in a straight rush seaward. That swift current was sending the *Delta Queen* downstream faster than before.

The river has always had a tendency to make cutoffs for itself. In the soft alluvial mud over which it travels, it tends to move in looping bends, after the manner of flowing watercourses everywhere in yielding earth. The bends grow deeper and finally cut through and meet at the loops. Then the river flows straighter for a while, leaving behind it a forgotten oxbow lake, a slough filling with lotuses and smartweeds, to mark where an old bend of the river was lost. The Mississippi, in all its millions of years of existence, has been making these bends and loops and cutoffs, in its own way, in its own time, for its own purposes.

This shortening process gave the government engineers the idea of doing the same thing, but doing it more efficiently. Why let a boat and tow go to all that work and use up so much fuel in shoving around a great bend when it was so much shorter to cut straight through? The prime example of wasted time was the old New Madrid Bend, which takes a boat twenty-one miles around, yet is only seven-tenths of a mile through the narrow part of the bend. The skilled engineers realized that the New Madrid Bend should be left as it was, its narrow neck revetted against a break-through, because the water would surge dangerously fast through such a cut. But there were many other bends below which could be fixed.

So, between 1929 and 1942, the energetic remodelers of the Mississippi directed sixteen cutoffs which would shorten the river by some 151 miles.

Yes, they shortened it; they made it more efficient, perhaps.

However, in the cuts, they have created roaring currents which rush downbound boats and tows too fast for safety, while, at the same time, they have produced a furious force for an upbound boat to push against. Sometimes this is so difficult for a boat with a heavy tow in high water, what with the danger of lines and wires breaking and setting barges dangerously adrift, that it must leave some of its barges tied to the bank below the cutoff. It must then take half of them above, tie them off and come back for the others in a tedious, time-taking, double-tripping operation which leaves nothing but low opinions and unflattering comments directed toward the men who made the cutoffs.

The Mississippi is normally and safely a wandering river, although the map of its valley is confusing. The river's travels have taken it not only north and south but also in its vast looping action east and west, cutting the great lateral bends. When these are shortened by natural or unnatural cutoffs, the river is often left in such a position that the state maps themselves are thrown into confusion. Because of this, parts of Arkansas are on the east bank, portions of Tennessee stranded over in Arkansas; pieces of Kentucky, Missouri and Tennessee are hopelessly jumbled, and parts of Mississippi are isolated on the wrong side of the river.

This unpredictable wandering, the river's hunger for new places and its insatiable taste for mud have caused certain river communities to vanish utterly from the maps, while others were perversely bypassed. Greenville, Mississippi, used to be on a bend of the river, but when the engineers made the Leland Cutoff and the Tarpley Cutoff, in 1933 and 1935, Greenville suddenly found itself on an oxbow lake and far from navigable river water.

For a river town, this is a serious situation. When the residents appealed for help, it was General Ferguson of the Corps of Engineers who solved the problem by opening a navigable channel below Greenville into the quiet lake that was left, thus connecting the town with the river again.

Greenville was thankful. It wanted to name the new lake-front river channel for the general, but he refused. He said it wasn't seemly for a place to be named for a living member of the armed forces. Thinking he was being merely modest, Greenville citizens wrote to the President himself, but he agreed with General Ferguson: it simply wasn't done. Greenville must find another name for its lake.

But the people of Greenville stubbornly called their precious waterfront Lake Ferguson anyway, and, if the government didn't approve, that was quite all right with Greenville. The government could name the lake whatever it chose.

But ever since, the Corps of Engineers, with no comment, has included Lake Ferguson on the annual navigation maps, with no mention at all about any illegality of the name.

Straight across this mixed-up river valley and a little north of where Greenville lies invisibly on the far-off eastern bank of its lake, there are now certain large and useless loops and bends which long ago carved the river landscape as the main channel of the Mississippi itself. At the most western point of the most western bend is Gaines Landing, which is still shown on the maps, though nothing lands there now except perhaps a few pirogues and the scows of fishermen going after catfish and gar. It is about nine miles due west of Greenville, about six from the main channel which the *Delta Queen* was navigating.

Extinct Island 81 is over there. It is an elderly island, lying miles from today's river, where all the islands are numbered, starting from the mouth of the Ohio and going south. Number 81 is indistinguishable from the land around it now, is really part of the land itself, but it is still numbered on the maps. Place names on the dead channel remain—Spanish Moss Bend,

Ashbrook Neck, Rowdy Bend.

These were the names by which the place was known a hundred years and more ago, when Gaines Landing was sometimes also called Far West Point, because it was as far west as the Lower Mississippi ever went. This was the channel of the river when Abraham Lincoln navigated his flatboat south; when Mark Twain piloted a steamboat; when General Grant's ironclads and converted steamboats went down to attack Vicksburg.

And it was here at Gaines Landing or Far West Point that covered wagons from the West came to meet the steamboats. They were caravans from far places, battered wagons out of the buffalo plains, and they were loaded with uncured hides but lately yanked bloodily from the bodies of millions of slaughtered bison.

Sometimes a thousand wagons loaded with hides were waiting. On a hot day, when a boat came down Ashbrook Neck, the pilot could smell what lay ahead, and if he didn't have the courage to face it, he might be tempted to turn his vessel around and go back. The green hides, if they had waited too long, putrified in the hot sun, yet they had to be loaded on a steamboat and taken to the tanneries before they spoiled. The steamboat crews had to steel themselves to attack the odoriferous task.

And today, the *Delta Queen*, miles east of Far West Point and Gaines Landing, and more than a hundred years removed from the dreadful wagons loaded with buffalo hides, moved rapidly down the man-made cutoffs of the Mississippi.

Greenville had its cutoff problems, and so did another river town, Vicksburg, face near disaster.

Vicksburg was strategically located at the top of what is probably the highest, steepest bluff on the Lower Mississippi. The roads which lead from the waterfront to the top of the town, even today, are some of the most precipitous pavements anywhere along the river, even including Galena, Natchez, or Alton.

During the War Between the States, Vicksburg was protected by that fortresslike hill, as well as by its incomparable view up and down the river and to the far western horizon. Any approaching vessel was detected at once and fired upon. General Grant wasted months in trying to cut a canal across a bend and bypass Vicksburg; but the river flooded, and the project was wrecked.

Grant and Sherman had tried to get at Vicksburg from up Chickasaw Bayou, tried to find a way down the Yazoo to the town's back door, and failed in every attempt. They could not attack from the river, but, instead, had to find a way of pushing in from the land side, and there they succeeded at last. After a seven-week siege of great horror and privation, Vicksburg fell.

And thirteen years later, the river itself, so long a friend, conquered the city with no trouble at all. In 1876 there was a flood and the swift current caused another cutoff. As a result, the Mississippi completely bypassed Vicksburg, leaving only a stagnant puddle where once had been a busy, well-defended waterfront. The new course was called Centennial Cut-off. It happened exactly one hundred years after 1776. To Vicksburg, it was a curse and a disaster. The town had only begun to revive following the war. And now this: no river—no commerce!

But not far away the Yazoo River still ran. It is said that a small boy was the one who suggested that a channel ought to be cut to connect the Yazoo on the north with the present course of the Mississippi, just south of Vicksburg—connect them so that the Yazoo would run along the Mississippi's old route past the town and enter that deserter river just below, providing a deep-water channel. And it worked!

River water now flows past Vicksburg, the green Yazoo River which churns into the mud of the Mississippi, showing a definite boundary line where the smaller stream enters the bigger one.

Below this is still another cutoff, an old one with a fascinating story related by Mark Twain. It was in 1848, the narrator said, when a cutoff was made at Raccourci Bend, below where Old River and the Atchafalaya today are trying to divert the Mississippi.

It was a wild and stormy night, and the water was rising fast. Old landmarks were gone, and the pilot of a certain steamboat couldn't see where the bars and shores and islands lay—it was all a dreadful blur of rain and storm and darkness, lit by vast sheets of lightning and rolling with thunder. But instead of tying up, the pilot continued, trying to see his way, and he turned down what he thought was the river channel. It *had* been the channel only yesterday, but it wasn't now—not any more. He was in a cutoff which was just beginning to form.

The pilot grew more and more excited and panicky. He knew there was something strange about the way things looked, but he didn't dare to tie up. It was too swampy, and the water was high; trees were falling over into the flood. And so there he was, knocking about in the old channel, trying to find the way out and not knowing that the river to the rear of the bend was filling up with sand and mud, cutting off retreat, and that the Mississippi had already cut through the neck above and closed the lower loop. So there was a lost steamboat, caught in Raccourci Old River, as it is called today. In his terrible alarm, the pilot cursed the storm, screaming that he wished to heaven he'd *never* get out of that confounded place. . . .

And, so the story goes, he never did. On stormy nights, that lost steamboat, like a ghostly *Flying Dutchman*, can still be seen and heard battering around in what is left of Raccourci Old River, forever lost and ever seeking.

Mark Twain could tell some good stories—rivermen today say he was a better storyteller than a pilot—but perhaps even he didn't hear about what happened to a steamboat in the early part of the twentieth century.

The steamer *Iron Mountain* left Vicksburg one day with ten loaded barges tied in front, and a full crew manning the vessel. The boat passed down a chute between an island and the mainland—and disappeared. The *Iron Mountain* never came out the other end of the chute and was never heard from again, neither she, nor her barges, nor her crew. The company which owned the steamboat finally wrote her off as lost and collected the insurance. The families of crew members mourned them as dead. But no one ever learned the secret of what happened to the *Iron Mountain*. Evidently it wasn't only haunted cutoffs and a master storyteller dedicated to the tales of the Mississippi which produced enduring mysteries. The Mississippi is still a strange and unfathomable river.

19. "And All the Night through Fog-Smoke White—"

Rain started by afternoon, and a good smell of wet willows came to the boat. Passengers, reluctant to miss the lovely, cool fragrance of the river in the rain, pushed their deck chairs under the canopies and roofs and stayed out of doors.

Flocks of black cormorants flew past. A herd of trim Nubian goats, brown and white, white and black, all white or all dark, went picking their way along the slant face of a broken concrete revetment, just above the water's edge. They went slowly, yet deliberately, as if they had a destination, and the people in their deck chairs leaned forward to watch and speculate on the curious little parade. The goats, like ladies in high-heeled slippers, were cautious, yet sure, choosing their way precisely, just above the lapping brown water. There was no sign of habitation, no people, no houses, only a herd of thirty-nine goats, walking along a revetment beside the quiet Mississippi.

The rain continued more heavily and by late afternoon almost everyone had had to retreat indoors, to the shelter of the comfortable lounges, until dinnertime. In the evening, there was a masquerade party, and while the dancing was in progress, the rain, which had been battering against the windows, slowed and stopped.

As soon as I stepped out into the coolness of the mist-wet deck, I knew that the *Delta Queen* had got out of the rain, only to run into fog. Thick fog. It enwrapped the boat, the distant music, the night, and gave everything an otherworldly quality which was all part of the mysterious river.

The far-off shores were dark against the webby mist which was boiling like steam from the water. The fog rose and swirled and moved and had life. It swathed an island, leaving only the willow tops thrusting out like peaks above cloud. The great searchlight, which was operated from the dark pilothouse, swung this way, swung that way, silently, probingly, reaching through the fog, cutting it like cheese—or finding a blank white solid through which it could not penetrate.

The light climbed above the fog level and, with a brilliant white glare rimmed with blue-purple, struck willow tops. It moved on, questioning, hunting . . . the eye of the steamboat at night, always seeking, suspicious of every dark spot, every shadow, every sudden silvery swirling of an eddy.

Out in that fog blanketing the steaming river lay the channel markers, the signposts of safe navigation. Without them, the pilot might as well tie up for the night. Even by day he required them as a guide to keep from running on to some hidden sand bar, ramming a sunken obstruction known only to the Corps of Engineers, or getting into shallow water, shoals, or rocks. Without visibility or markers, the *Delta Queen* would be in almost as much danger as any of the steamboats of the less well guarded Steamboat Era.

The black and white flat-topped buoys were on the right of the downbound boat, the pointed red and white nun buoys on the left. Except in very high water, boats must contrive to pass between them, for there and there alone lies the safe channel—and security. With the present high stage of water on the Ohio and the Mississippi, this was not quite so neces- sary by day when our pilot could see his way, but at night it was. The dim sparks of blinking shore lights guided the *Queen's* pilot as he steered toward one that was straight ahead on a bend, then steered toward the next, and the next. But the fog made these lights less visible, and he had a harder time finding them.

The mist was endlessly in motion, forever streaming toward the boat, filling the beam of the searchlight with millions of racing white particles, like fine snow, particles not tangible enough to be felt or touched or captured, yet strong enough to stop a boat. This was the spirit of the river, the condensa- tion of its moving and breathing and talking, of the living and dying going on within its restless, murky waters.

The lights and buoys grew more difficult to find. The *Delta Queen* might have to tie up to some willow-rooted bank and wait until the fog lifted. Old-time steamboat captains in a like situation often bluffed it out by setting the deck hands to beating on tin pans and ringing bells. The clatter announced that a steamboat was charging blindly down the river.

Still, this fog was not yet too dense, not too impervious to light . . . not yet. The beam reached out again and slanted down from the heights of the big vessel, down to where the water was, only the fog would not let it be seen. There the light caught the form of a big, drifting tree, slimy with scum, lolloping along half concealed in the water. But it missed the boat and the big paddle wheel and went on.

There came an opening in the vapor, like a clear pool in the walling whiteness, and there was the sudden, reassuring reflection of a red nun buoy, calling silently "this is the way, follow me."

The light swung to the right, still hunting, found a black and white can buoy. Captain Hampton knew he was heading correctly if he went straight down between the two buoys, but that when he got between them, he must immediately send his finger of light onward, to find the next buoy. Then he must find the next light, blinking like a large, persistent firefly at the edge of the willows, and the next and the next and the next, all night long, or as long as the night and the fog would let him.

There was a sudden clearing. The clouds broke, and the stars in a black sky looked through. In patches of open river they were reflected like pinpoints of eternal light, only to be lost again, like drifting silver minnows, in a river of mist. Now, as suddenly as it had opened up, the white wall closed in ahead, so firmly that the light met only a barrier. The cottony structure was deceptively frail and delicate, yet quite impervious to the thrust of light. It might completely conceal an approaching boat or an unknown obstacle.

The pilot blew the fog whistle, three long blasts and then three more, cautiously nosing into the mass of mist. He heard no answering blast. Apparently, no boat was ahead. There must be a pair of buoys out there, but Captain Hampton could not find them. He rang the indicator to the engine room, pushed back the throttle and slowed the *Queen* to a crawl, blatting her mournful fog whistle, backing water so that her wake churned like violent cream in the fog and starshine and searchlight glow. The whistle was a spine-tingling distress call—

"I am lost in fog . . . I am lost in fog . . . stay out of my way . . . *blast* . . . *blast* . . . *blast*. . . ."

The boat was headed slowly toward the dark shore, which loomed indistinctly, the searchlight full on it now, hunting a willow to which she might tie.

And then, just as suddenly as it had enveloped boat and river, the fog opened once more, as a wind came upstream and blew the mist quite away for a time. The *Delta Queen* resumed speed, now that the buoys were clearly lit ahead, the shore lights briskly twinkling. The men in the pilothouse and engine room were congratulating themselves at having outwitted the fog, the deck crew thankful they had not been called, after all, to get out on a strange shore to tie up the boat . . . when the fog-dragon came menacing again.

It was nearly midnight when, suddenly, around a bend, there lay a solid wall of white. The *Queen* again slowed, and the light punched and probed and thrust and could not get through, could not find the buoys, could not even find the shore of the state of Mississippi. Everything was white now, like the inside of a Dakota blizzard. The stars were blotted out. The men on the late watch came on deck. It always happened like this, they were muttering philosophically, *they* were always the ones who got the fog to tie up in. The young first mate, Doc Hawley, had his men ready with lines.

The whistle bellowed defeat. The pilot slowly, carefully, shoved the big boat around in a half circle, to run her head into the bank of the Louisiana shore.

"Right in here," hollered the mate. "We're all right. We're at Hole-in-Wall Plantation, Cap. Take it easy now. . . ."

The boat pushed in gently against the sheer mudbank. The roots of the trees growing there were hanging over the water, which had washed away the soil and would eventually pull them in with a relentless grasp. The second deck was on a level with the top of the high bank. The Negro deck hands, in their orange life jackets with the luminous patches lit up by the searchlights, waited, shivering, then gingerly went over a narrow plank to shore, tied a line around a tree and a stern line aft. The stern line pulled loose, the willow going with it.

"Pick out a *big* tree!" shouted the captain. "Tie on to one that'll hold, can't you?"

The engines quieted, the searchlights went out, a light snapped on in the pilothouse as the pilot got out his logbook and checked the time of tying up. And the big paddle wheel still revolved lazily as the river's current moved it, casting drops back into the dark whiteness until it finally slowed to a stop, dripping. The drops, in the sudden silence, cast themselves noisily into the black and moving water.

Everyone went to bed except the watchmen, faithfully making their rounds, while fog particles misted on the decks and railings. A chuck-will's-widow, somewhere in the woods on shore, uttered the deep, staccato coughing which was its song.

At six o'clock in the morning, the *Delta Queen* was still tied up to the bank outside Hole-in-Wall Plantation. Industrious spiders had worked all night in the fog to build webs among the willows on shore. Many a fragile silken line was connected to the boat itself, while nets hung between lifeboat and post. The webs that ornamented the iron grilling now, at dawn, were beginning to sparkle with pale, sunlit drops of fog-dew.

Birds were awake on the bank and in the willow oaks, singing with the fervor of a Louisiana spring morning. A Carolina wren, a plump, cinnamon-brown little bird with a white eyebrow, had come aboard the *Delta Queen* and was intently nipping up spiders below the teakwood railings. The crew scrubbing down the decks advanced steadily with hose, brooms, and brushes; so, with a final rolling burst of song, the wren flitted down into the woods.

Somewhere in the murk, a rooster was crowing over and over again. On the packed mud of the bank lay festoons of dewberry vines in full flower, garlands of stars against the dark mud.

The fog was moving now, lifting, parting, vanishing, and the pilot could see well enough to proceed. The *Delta Queen* was an hour or so above Natchez. The men untied the lines and dragged them aboard, the wheel revolved, and the steamboat circled out into the water and headed downstream once more. By the time the chime boy came around, playing his softly musical, insistent getting-up tune, the fog had broken and lifted, except for white pockets in ravines on the high shore. Birds sang, and a little wind kicked up modest white caps which gave an air of excitement to the river.

20. Natchez

The *Delta Queen* nosed cautiously up to the muddy waterfront below the big bluff of Natchez, Mississippi, and stopped. The landing stage was put out to meet an old concrete road which came steeply down to end in the river itself. This was once the precipitous way to the ferry, replaced a few years ago by a bridge.

Little of old Natchez on the top of the bluff was visible from the clotted mud of the shore, from the tangled willows and debris at the mooring. But the sound of the landing whistle roused people in the unpainted, ramshackle, old houses a quarter of the way up the bluff. Those who heard, quickly scrambled out of bed. Tousled heads were thrust from windows. Negro children scampered out on rickety porches.

"There's the steamboat," they were all saying. "Steamboat's come in early—what-all we goin' to sell the folks?"

The weedy wasteland of that waterfront and the shacks on the slope gave little notion of a place which has been a point of habitation among white men for two hundred and fifty years, and by Indians for perhaps thousands of years.

It was the Natchez Indians—or their ancestors—who found this spot first. Knowing the river's habit of climbing periodically into the lowlands and flooding everything for miles, they chose for their town and for the home of the chief this sheer bluff rising majestically above the river.

The Mississippi gnawed at the yellow-brown earth, was forever crumbling and dissolving bits of it into the moving water, but White Apple Village of the Natchez and the people themselves would vanish before the bluff went away. White Apple was, indeed, secure from the river—but not from the Frenchmen who coveted it.

The Natchez Indians were tall, well built, proud and insolent people. They may have been descended from the more remote tribes who built mounds along the rivers, the Hopewellians, or perhaps from the conquering Mississippians. These ancient people were sun worshipers, and so were the Natchez.

Their chief was called the Great Sun, kinsman of that sacred orb which rose each day, climbed the sky and sank beyond the river at nightfall. The Great Sun himself, in holy isolation, lived on the temple mound where, on the altar, stood a reed basket containing the bones of the previous Great Sun. These would be removed only when the present chief died and joined his ancestor on the altar. But the last of the Great Suns of the Natchez was not to be permitted to have his remains placed on the sacred temple mound.

The French, settling Louisiana, building miserable towns at Mobile and Biloxi and New Orleans, wanted forts up the Mississippi to provide safety from northern attack. They had the whole Mississippi Valley and many vantage points on the hills to choose from, but they selected the bluff containing White Apple Village and the temple mound.

The Sieur de Bienville boldly erected a fort not far from the rim of the bluff, just above where the *Delta Queen* was moored, and named it Fort Rosalie, in honor of the beautiful and elegant Duchess de Pontchartrain. The fort was neither beautiful nor elegant. It was beset with mosquitoes, heat, humidity, wind, an ever-encroaching jungly forest—and a horde of angry and increasingly resentful Indians who lived not far away.

The French had given the Natchez an ultimatum: sell White Apple Village or be destroyed—and have the village taken, anyway. The canny Natchez chieftain had pondered this deeply. Then he begged—very humbly indeed for a Natchez, which should have put the Intendant immediately on his guard, but did not—that he and his people might have the space of two moons in which to find a new location for their village, and to move the bones of the honored Great Sun to another suitably sanctified resting place. The tall, bronzed Natchez bowed deeply and looked down meekly when he said this, and the French Intendant thought the savage was being very reasonable and accommodating. It would certainly do no harm to wait for two months, if trouble and bloodshed could thus be averted.

But, as soon as the Natchez knew that they had time in which to prepare for what they intended to do, they immediately went into action. It was at this period that other tribes in the Lower Mississippi Valley also were seething from French invasion, conquest and injustice. Not only the Natchez but the Choctaws, Yazoos, Chickasaws, Tunicas and others were full of fury. Three tribal groups got together at last, although they had warred on each other often enough. They made a decision on a course of action which, they felt, would get rid of the French permanently, wipe them off the lovely Mississippi landscape forever. This included burning the odious, ugly fort so that no vestige remained to mark where it had stood.

Normally, the Natchez would not have chosen to ally themselves with anyone, much less the people they considered their inferiors, the Choctaws and Yazoos, but they knew that, in this crisis, they needed concerted action from many points. Only by enlisting other tribes could their objective be accomplished.

The last day of November, 1729, would be the date for the massacre of the French. Since the Indians had no calendars, they needed to keep track of exactly how many days lay between the conclave and the attack itself. A slave was sent down to the river side, where, in the nearest canebrake, he cut a bundle of straight cane stalks. The leaves were peeled off, and the clean rods were presented to the Natchez chief in a neat bundle. Slowly, three separate bundles were counted out, each containing the same number of rods, one for each day. The two other chiefs went home with their rods and gave them to the head priests in their towns.

Each morning, the head priest was to take out one cane stalk and burn it. When there was only one left, it meant that the next day was the one appointed for striking the blow against the intruders. The Yazoos and Natchez would attack Fort Rosalie, the Choctaws would strike New Orleans. They would all attack simultaneously, with violence, completely surprising their victims who, before they could recover and defend themselves, would all be dead.

It is said that the mother of the Natchez chief was a friend of the French; this is difficult to believe, but the stories say it was so. And this woman, learning the secret of the mysterious bundle of canes in the priest's house, slipped in one night and took out two of the rods. By her reasoning, in thus

advancing the time when the Natchez would attack Fort Rosalie, the other tribes would not be at their designated places to help carry out the unified plot against the French. In this way the New Orleans people would be warned in time to arm and prepare before the Choctaws struck.

The Natchez head priest, apparently unaware of what had happened, announced two days ahead that the time had indeed come. And on a dark, dripping, lowering day in late November, without waiting for the mysteriously absent Yazoos, the Natchez attacked Fort Rosalie. They swarmed up the walls, burned, killed—they killed everyone they could lay hands on, women and little children, in addition to the men—all but a handful of people who escaped and, almost crazed, made their way to warn New Orleans.

As a result, New Orleans managed to fend off the Choctaw attack. Whereupon, the Choctaws and Yazoos were furious at what they felt was typical Natchez duplicity. They turned against their one-time allies. The French were also pursuing the Natchez into the back country.

There followed a series of bloody battles, during a pursuit that lasted a year. This reprisal action was sufficient to break the Natchez completely. Together with the silent Great Sun, a thousand captive Natchez in chains were taken down the river to New Orleans, where most of those who survived were shipped to Santo Domingo as slaves.

The French did not hold the Natchez bluff and the fort for very long, however. The area became British by 1764, and the English flag flew over the fort, now called Fort Panmure, until 1779. Then Spain took it over, but for only nineteen years did the Spanish flag dominate the Natchez bluff, with its all-but-forgotten White Apple Village site and the deserted temple mound. In 1798, Natchez became American.

With the growth of river travel, the city on the bluff became a trading center, a market to which men in boats of all sorts came from up or down the river, to sell or exchange goods brought from far places. Steamboats, flatboats, rafts, and keelboats were lined up for several miles where only the *Delta Queen* stops today. For many years, Natchez was the farthest northern point of civilization up the river valley from New Orleans. Around it gathered rich plantations, many of whose owners built their homes in the city itself.

From the Spanish occupation, through the rising opulence of the years before the War Between the States, the magnificence of Natchez grew and flourished. Some of the most beautiful homes in America were erected here among some of the loveliest gardens and under some of the biggest live oaks and magnolias in the South. Gracious living was easy when slave labor could be expected to take care of the ugliness, the hard work, the daily drudgery of housekeeping and gardening. Life among the white people in the big homes and plantations of Natchez could indeed be fine and beautiful.

The homes were given names—Airlie, Greenwood, Dun-
leith, D'Evereaux, Arlington, Choctaw, Cherokee, The Elms,
and so on. Many of them had splendid Doric or Corinthian
pillars, either across the front or all the way around. The
interiors had exquisite floors, rugs, woodwork; crystal chan-
deliers of great magnificence which had come from France;
velvet draperies, snowy muslin curtains; hand-rubbed furniture imported from England; the finest of everything. Staircases attained the perfection of intricately hung curves and
spirals. Ceilings were decorated with bas reliefs in plaster.

Though many of the homes were more simple, even these
had an air of quiet elegance. But there was always the contrast of wealth with poverty, freedom with slavery, beauty
with ugliness. There were the houses called haunted, mansions
that knew murders, ghosts of maidens blighted in love, oaks
under which men dueled to the death.

All this was on top of the hill. Below, down on old Silver
Street, lay Natchez-Under-the-Hill where the boats came in,
where run-down shacks and waterfront shanties housed the
gamblers, the murderers, the thieves, criminals and other low
characters. These either came in on the boats or lived at
Natchez-Under-the-Hill solely to prey upon strangers and
profit by the wealth coming in on keelboat, flatboat and steamboat.

Sometimes there was retaliation: quick, hot gunfire in the
night, swords flashing, a dagger between ribs, a quiet splash
in the moving brown waters of the Mississippi.

Or, as happened once—and perhaps oftener, who knows?—
an irate steamboat captain, upon demanding money back from
one of the local swindlers and being refused with considerable insolence, quietly tied a line from his boat to the supports
of the frail, waterfront shack housing the villain.

"Now, give me my money!" demanded the captain. "Or I
shall order full speed astern and pull you and this miserable

shanty into the river!"

The boat gave an experimental, warning tweak, which made the unstable structure shudder, and the swindler, pale to the eyebrows, hastily emerged. He thrust his ill-gotten money into its rightful owner's outstretched hand.

"Quick, untie your infernal boat, will you, before you pull everything into the river!"

"Not until you give me the rest of your money," said the captain calmly, while the steamboat puffed. "I know you got it wrongfully, so you might as well hand it over!"

Not until the swindler was cleaned out did the captain untie the line. The steamboat turned with a wash of waves into the river and headed away from the old landing on Silver Street.

Silver Street has long since been eaten up by the river, and with it went all the shanties and gambling dens and other iniquitous places which distinguished Natchez-Under-the-Hill. The *Delta Queen* had landed in the deep water which now covers all that remains of the unlamented place.

Natchez had crime at its front door and at its back. It is a wonder that the city ever survived at all, or that it could be so beautiful in between. Coming into the rear of the city from the northeast was the Natchez Trace. This was the overland route connecting New Orleans with Natchez, and on to Nashville, Louisville and the Ohio River. The Trace was originally an Indian trail, and it was never safe, even to Indians. Too many different tribes living along its length resented trespassers.

When white men began traveling it, the Trace became even more dangerous and notorious. When a man set out to go a distance on that road, he was never sure of being seen again. If travelers got through successfully from the east, they ended their trip thankfully at King's Tavern, at the east side of Natchez, and set about to eat, drink, rest—and tell bloody tales of hairbreadth escapes.

Or an incoming traveler might have a smug, well-heeled look and not talk much. He would be one of those who had lain in wait along the Trace, as did Samuel Mason, the bloody Harpes, and many another ferocious character.

The old Natchez Trace is still an indelible mark on the American landscape, connecting invisible steamboat trails on the rivers with the more permanent patterns of man's travels on land. Near Natchez, it has been so deeply impressed into the yielding loess, whose sheer banks are overgrown with honeysuckle and bordered by oaks with boughs which meet overhead and long gray moss hanging low and shadowy, that the road is far beneath the level of the surrounding earth. It was thus, even in its earlier days, a perfect place for an ambush. Even now, one feels the unseen menace of the past, the drama of lone travelers along this quiet, beautiful, flower-fragrant, deadly trail connecting the rivers.

After breakfast, we went ashore. Taxis, cars and buses came down the precipitous road to pick up those who had arranged to take a tour of five of the Natchez homes. The Natchez Pilgrimage itself had been over for a week, but ladies of the Garden Club had arranged to open some of the homes and gardens especially for these appreciative guests.

A storm the day before had beaten the irises low, had scattered quantities of pink, white, flame and scarlet azalea flowers on the ground beneath the still-laden bushes; a good many luscious camellias had fallen off, too, but the flowers of Natchez still looked wonderful to the northern eyes which had come to see springtime in the South.

Thick Spanish moss, still dripping moisture, hung from the magnolias and live oaks, adding to that romantic look one associates with the Old South and ancient Natchez. On the bluff's rim, down below where old Fort Rosalie used to stand before the Indians attacked it, grew big Paulownia or princess trees, with their large purple trumpet blossoms massed on furry, golden-brown twigs. With few leaves visible as yet, the Paulownias looked, from a distance, like trees full of wisteria flowers. They were much sought, that April morning, by the Natchez bees.

There must have been a mockingbird on every chimney of the old pillared houses, as well as on those of the little old houses along Buckeye Alley and the back lanes, and they were all exuberant with song in the sunshine that poured over them after the rain and fog. As I explored Natchez on foot, from north to south and from the eastern edge to the river bluff, I had a chorus of mockingbird song accompanying me wherever I went. Hundreds of migrant birds, passing up the Mississippi, had paused to sing and feed in Natchez gardens. Among azaleas and rain-wet camellias, the gardens were a jumble of song.

The city was a combination of old and new, with the past predominating where the houses stood in their lovely overgrown gardens; the new visible in modern streets and downtown buildings. Yet pervading the atmosphere subtly, in spite of bird song and the gracious beauty of flowers and old homes and great trees, somewhere, somehow, the remembrance of those proud, bronze-skinned earlier Natchez people was always present. There was always the lurking memory of the Great Sun on his temple mound each morning, saluting his kinsman, the sun . . . the screams of the French dying in Fort Rosalie, in that place not far from where the stately mansion called Rosalie now placidly stands, with the purple Paulownia trees behind it. The bandits punctuating the Natchez Trace with blood; the carousing and gunfire of the wild waterfront of old Silver Street; the War, when Union forces cut down some of the ancient oaks of Natchez for firewood and desecrated gardens and homes . . . they are all here, and so is the ghostly line-up of forgotten steamboats at the waterfront, where the *Delta Queen* alone lay waiting for us to come down the steep hill in time for lunch. The distant past of Natchez is never very far away.

21. Twenty-eight Oaks

A long time ago, perhaps almost two hundred years ago, though no one will know for certain until an oak tree dies and its growth rings are counted, an unknown French colonist built a cabin several hundred yards away from the Mississippi's west bank. The Frenchman had come with splendid hopes of becoming a great planter, to build a fine house and create around it beautiful gardens and big trees, such as he had seen and admired on the great estates in France. In the New World all things were possible. The land was rich, the climate tropical, rain abundant, and life must be at its best.

To begin with, he built a modest French-Provincial house, promising his wife to build a better one soon. And, to set the stage for the great estate he hoped to develop, he planted a double row of live oak trees, twenty-eight trees, so widely spaced apart that it was inconceivable that they would ever grow big enough to fill all that space. The avenue was ninety feet wide, and the diminutive oaks looked puny and just a little ridiculous, lining up from the front yard of the small house with its high-pitched roof all the way to the river's edge.

The unknown Frenchman planted his fields, put in a good crop of indigo and a little sugar; but the caterpillars got the indigo, and the sugar did not do well. For several years after that, the crops were failures. Sickness came to his family and his wife died, and then his children. At last the man, in grief and desperation, went away from the place, which seemed to be cursed, and no one knows what became of him.

The little house and sheds and barn finally fell to pieces. They were finished off when a hurricane swept in from the Gulf of Mexico. But the young live oak trees were too young and too resilent to break. They whipped about in the gale, but when it was over, they still stood: twenty-eight oaks in a double line, far apart from each other.

It was not until the 1830's that anyone else came to claim that land. At that time, Jacques Télesphore Roman acquired the tract containing the twenty-eight oaks. He wanted it particularly because of the trees. He loved the out of doors, was most happy when he was walking beneath the great trees of Louisiana, hunting in the Louisiana prairies that stretched to Texas, fishing in the bayous, or just sitting on the river-bank, watching the Mississippi flow past.

It was Jacques Roman and his wife who decided to put a noble house at the far end of the avenue of oaks. The trees had grown much, but they were still young in stature as com-pared with many on the great plantations of Louisiana. Still, they had possibilities, and each year they put out more growth. Already, the arching boughs were stretching out toward each other, across the wide-spaced avenue.

The house was built in 1836, a square brick and stucco man-sion of a soft buffy pink, with twenty-eight Doric columns all around it. Jacques Roman wanted to keep the pattern of twenty-eight—in his trees, in his columns, even in the number of slave cottages which later sprang up back of the big house.

The owners named the beautiful pink house Bon Séjour— Good Rest—and so it was, especially to Jacques Roman, to whom it was the embodiment of all that was lovely in Louisiana. Its long, floor-length windows opened out to the wide gallery on all sides. Whenever he wished, he could step out into the gardens, out to the orange trees, out to see where his slave, Antoine, was producing the first successful grafts of pecan trees; out to the formal gardens, or to the long, arching avenue of oaks, beyond which lay a glimmer of the Mississippi.

This was sugar country, and sugar was the coming thing. Men and plantations grew rich with the sweet crop, and Bon Séjour was among them. More and more, the plantation with its incomparable pink house at the end of the growing avenue of oaks became known as Oak Allée. Passing steamboats slowed for passengers to take a quick look, for the trees shut out any view of the house until one was exactly at the avenue's end and could gaze far ahead, three hundred yards from the river, at what appeared to be a miniature pink house with pillars framed in trees.

The War Between the States ruined the Romans. They departed from Bon Séjour and others took it over, let it grow shabby and unrepaired. At last, the once-fine house stood empty, mouldering in the Louisiana atmosphere which so quickly reduces elegance to dust. Not until about 1917 was any thought given to saving the house, and then only the roof was repaired, to keep out rain. A few years later, Mr. and Mrs. Andrew Stewart bought Oak Allée Plantation.

It was a long, painstaking job to restore the elegance of the old house to what it was before ruin set in, but it was accomplished at last. The house had indeed begun to decay, but not the trees which had been planted long ago by an unknown Frenchman with ideals of glory. Even he could hardly have known what he did when he planted those trees—though perhaps maybe he did, at that. He had seen the old live oaks in Louisiana, had seen how tremendously they spread their branches, even though the height of the trees was not always as great as the width. Why else had he planted his little saplings so far apart, with that immense, ninety-foot avenue lying between? For today the oaks have extended their huge, reptilian boughs all the way across the avenue. They meet and interlock overhead. The trunks have a circumference of twenty-one feet. And not one of the twenty-eight has died.

On a cool, rainy morning, the *Delta Queen* slid quietly up to a green levee-landing on the west bank of the river, down in the Evangeline Country of Louisiana. This is also called the Cajun Country, a name derived from those Acadian refugees, of whom Evangeline was one, who came from Nova Scotia in 1755.

The *Queen* tied up to the bank—and as she did so, we saw what we had been waiting to see. Exactly abreast of it, we beheld the great avenue of twenty-eight oaks of Oak Allée, old Bon Séjour and the pink-buff pillars of the big house, blurred in the rain, at the far end.

At the first sound of the boat's whistle, a large black and white dog came hurrying along the corridor of oaks. He leaped down the shell path over the levee and assaulted with joy the members of the crew already on the bank, where they were arranging the landing stage. The dog cavorted about and licked the hands of the deck crew, tried to jump on the dangling landing stage as it was being maneuvered down, so that he could hurry aboard at once.

This was Spot, the overseer's dog, the self-appointed welcoming committee to the hospitality of Oak Allée. Although Spot had not seen the *Delta Queen* since the previous autumn, he had not forgotten. He was eager to get aboard the steamboat, greet the night watchman, the purser and the captain, the head deck hand and his assistants, and then go quietly, his manners finished, to the galley for a handout.

Spot accompanied us on our walk up the levee and to the gate and beneath the incredible, arching trees, after which he vanished.

The oaks formed a majestic colonnade of trees. The young leaves were just coming out, while the old leaves still remained. The latter live about thirteen months, which gives the annual new growth time to mature before the old falls off. The live oak is thus never bare; it always presents to the world the look of an evergreen tree. The Frenchman who planted them would be overwhelmed to see them now.

Yet, there seemed to be something that was missing, something which Longfellow mentioned:

> ". . . oaks, from whose branches
> Garlands of Spanish moss. . . ."

There was no Spanish moss on the trees at Oak Allée. Elsewhere in Louisiana, oaks of this size would be heavily draped with it, like the old Packenham oaks down at Versailles Plantation, and at D'Estréhan and in the swamps . . . everywhere.

But at Oak Allée there is none because the owners keep it carefully picked off. The boys are sent up into the broad branches to remove the gray tendrils as soon as any may appear. There is some controversy as to whether or not Spanish moss actually hurts trees, but the owners of Oak Allée are taking no chances on their priceless trees. Thus there is a long, open, arching green cavern of an avenue leading under trees from the levee gate to the house. Only the masses of little dark green resurrection ferns and pale gray lichens upholster the big, horizontal boughs.

The avenue led to the front portico with its enormous pillars twined with wisteria, and giant yucca plants holding pyramids of cream-colored flowers as high as the second-floor gallery. As guests of Oak Allée, we were ushered into the broad central hall, to be greeted by the owner herself, Mrs. Josephine Armstrong Stewart. We were then escorted through the charming old rooms, upstairs and down. Great blue Chinese jars held masses of sweet-olive branches with their highly perfumed greenish flowers, while out of doors, in the garden, more of that exotic perfume called to us.

It was a mingling of many scents—orange trees in bloom and the fragrance of the sweet-olive bushes, and roses, irises, scarlet lilies. Purple trumpets on the allamanda vines climbing up into the palmettoes hung dripping with moisture. There was a junglelike thicket of bamboo, which should have entertained a tiger or a boa constrictor, at least, but seemed devoid of any life except for some small skittering lizards. Banana trees were starting to put up new growth. There were massive caladium leaves, five feet wide, down which raindrops trickled . . . the beautiful haunts of a Louisiana garden more than a hundred years old.

But the atmosphere of the past was shattered by something beyond the old house and its trees and gardens. Out there were pastures—pastures studded matter-of-factly with hundreds of large brown cattle. From a distance, they appeared to be about as big as buffalo. These were animals which did not belong to the past at all, but to the present and to the future. They were Santa Gertrudis cattle whose breed was not acknowledged as a separate variety until 1940.

The Acadian farmers in Louisiana two hundred years ago had kept cattle. The moist Louisiana prairies held good pastureland, but ticks, drouth, heat and disease were hard on cows accustomed to a more northern climate, and many died.

Through all the years that lie between the early Cajuns and the Stewart Ranch of today, spread dauntless hours of experimentation, of loss, of trying again and again to find the kind of cattle which would not only survive but thrive in this demanding climate and landscape. It was the sturdy, disease- and heat-resistant Brahmas, those humped, flop-eared, pale gray sacred cows of India, experimented with in Florida, Louisiana and Texas, which seemed especially adapted for southern pastures in the United States.

In Texas, the King Ranch successfully crossed the Brahma with the brown shorthorn. The resultant perfected species was named the Santa Gertrudis. It had the short, conical horns and red-brown color of the shorthorn, and the sleek, loose hide, the stocky build, great size, heavy meat and resistance to heat and sun and disease of the big sacred Brahma, minus the hump, long horns and ferocious disposition. These were cattle which had been made to order for the hot, humid, tick-infested lands along the Gulf of Mexico and the Lower Mississippi.

The Armstrong Ranch in Texas adjoins the tremendous King Ranch, and is second only to the latter as a breeder of fine Santa Gertrudis animals. Under the guidance of Armstrong-Stewart methods, great numbers of these superb cattle are raised on the Stewart Ranch near Vacherie, Louisiana, at Oak Allée Plantation.

To stand dreamily on the gallery of an elegant ante-bellum home in a gentle spring rain, and to smell orange blossoms and the mould of centuries, and to see the little brown lizards skittering up the bamboo stalks and ferns greening on the arching arms of ancient oaks—and then to look beyond to the modern pastures with these ultramodern cattle, is to skip too fast from one world to another.

Yet, this up-to-date ranch and the Santa Gertrudises it produces are one of the saving solutions to the crumbling hopes and dynasties of the Old South.

For a long time, the South could not adapt to the present but only mourned the past, so it met a lingering decay in trying to live stubbornly back in old days lost beyond recall.

Now the South has come alive, and the river has largely done it—not only with fine cattle grazing on its lowlands, but with oil and sugar refineries, ranged for miles along its banks, and the industries springing from both businesses, plus chemicals, sulphur, turpentine, lumber, tung oil, pecans, rice and shrimp. A profitable international trade has resulted from the booming businesses along the Mississippi with its sheltered harbors. The New South is a wonder to behold. It is not only managing successfully to retain the gracious, impractical aspects of its beautiful past (as in Oak Allée plantation and many more along the River Road), it is also managing to progress and live and prosper in a modern world.

Only the night before, we had passed Baton Rouge, which in itself is an example of success. Just above the city, at Profit Island, the *Delta Queen* had met deep water, had almost reached sea level. In the darkness, we had been unaware of any island, but were fascinated by the magnificence of Baton Rouge at night, with its multitude of lights on the capitol, the oil refineries and the many ships tied up there. It is much prettier and more dramatic to pass most river cities at night, especially Baton Rouge.

The oil refineries are occupied by strangely beautiful, exciting structures which are, in practical terms, the catcrackers, the fractionating towers, the hydrogenating units, the spherical and ovoid and cheesebox-shaped tanks for butane, propane and high octane gasolines and other products. They are the result of separating from the dark, thick, smelly crude oil which comes in by pipeline and tanker from Louisiana and Texas the many parts which compose it—high and low octane gasolines, kerosene, Diesel oil and asphalt, plus the gases and chemicals which also come from that magic liquid mineral.

The oil refinery is a blaze of glory at night. Every structure is brilliantly outlined. Like the pleasure concessions of a fair, lights top their crowns and towers, their ladders and platforms. Meanwhile, the orange fires of exhaust gas flare into the night wind, and smoke and steam, lit by the glow, billow upward in high drama. Passing a large refinery at night is one of the exciting things to see from the river.

As pointed out, at Baton Rouge there are not only the myriads of reflected lights in the sliding black water, but also those on the big tankers and freighters tied up to the deep-water docks. The tall column of the capitol has a shaft of white light pointing down to the grave of the assassinated governor, Huey P. Long.

Night closed in darker than ever when we were finally past all the glow and glory. We went to bed that night looking forward to our arrival at New Orleans late the next day.

22. New Orleans

The *Delta Queen* was still ahead of schedule. The big, wide, flooding river had carried her speedily to her goal. Instead of docking at New Orleans about midnight on Friday, she came triumphantly around the big curve of the old river city at two o'clock in the afternoon.

She passed the "boneyard of forgotten steamboats"—the old Bisso Shipyard with its partially dismantled, mouldering vessels which once had proudly sailed the river. It was as depressing a sight as an automobile junk yard, and as unhandsome. Bent old smokestacks, shattered decks, broken railings, a mélange of discarded relics of the past lay huddled along the New Orleans upper shore. Nearer to the main part of the city, however, the sturdy old steam ferry, the *Thomas Pickles*, with her two tall black chimneys, known on the river since 1896, was loading cars and passengers at the

New Orleans bank, to cross to Algiers.

Algiers, Louisiana, is the old town built originally of lumber brought down the river in the form of flatboats, a hundred and forty years ago. The French in New Orleans romantically called this new town across the river Algiers because it reminded them of how Algiers in Africa lay across the Mediterranean from France.

From the *Delta Queen*, we could begin to make out the distant steeples of St. Louis Cathedral, could see the city roofs stretching behind the endless line of wharf boats and banana-loading docks, where the white fruit boats, by means of endless-belt conveyors, were unloading tons of green bananas. There were coffee boats flying South American flags. The line-up of merchant shipping—Japanese freighters, Norwegian craft, Swedish vessels, tankers from Liberia, ships from Liverpool and Amsterdam and Bruges,—extended in an exciting curve, as far as could be seen down the river.

They lay where once lay the magnificent line-up of steamboats, all with their heads pointing at an angle to the bank, raising a forest of smokestacks against the sky. It was a patterned sky in the old days, not only with steamboats and their tall chimneys but with the great masts and spars and rigging of sailing vessels in from far ports. And lying below, inconspicuous but important, too, in the story of New Orleans, were tied up the big flatboats and keelboats which had come with great loads of Middle Western products from more than a thousand miles away.

This was the place where the *Natchez* and the *Robert E. Lee* detached themselves from the steamboat line-up and set off on a nation-shaking race. In their wheel-wash, passing along an equally exciting line-up of ships, the *Delta Queen* slowed her own progress, seeking her landing.

But we were not on the only steamboat left, not the *Delta Queen* nor the sturdy old *Thomas Pickles* and the dismal boneyard of the lost boats at Bisso's. The big excursion steamer *President*, owned by the Streckfus Lines, which also operate the *Admiral* at St. Louis, came upstream as if to meet the *Queen*. This was flattering, but the truth was that the *President* was just setting out on her daily two-and-one-half hour cruise along the waterfront of New Orleans, and we met.

The *President* is the same length as the *Delta Queen* and was built in 1924 as a fine packet originally called the *Cincinnati*. But when hard times hit the remaining packets, the side-wheeler was sold to Streckfus, which remodeled the vessel, removed her staterooms and reintroduced her to the rivers on the Fourth of July, 1934, as a deluxe excursion boat. She can, and usually does, carry some three thousand persons on afternoon and evening trips.

As the two steamboats passed each other, people aboard the *President* took pictures of the *Delta Queen*, while all the camera equipment on the *Delta Queen* was brought into play to snap the passing *President*. We were mutually interesting to each other. At the same time that our purser was explaining over the public address system about the *President*, a similar explanation of the *Delta Queen* was taking place on the excursion steamer, audible across the waters. So, with mutual congratulations and esteem and a saluting of whistles, the two went on, one, a side-wheel, the other stern wheel, both filled almost to capacity with relaxed, delighted passengers in an age of jet travel, fast trains, motor cars . . . two old steamboats busily plying the Mississippi and doing very well at it.

Nearing the wharves, the *Delta Queen* blew a long, sonorous landing whistle, complete with echoes, and with the sound of it bouncing against the dock buildings and startling the gulls lined up on the roofs, there was a certain lifting of our hearts, a thrill of triumph. The Big Lady had reached her goal!

She slid neatly into her berth between a shabby, dull orange and maroon Norwegian freighter in need of paint and a snappy black and white Japanese freighter called the *Takai Maru,* riding high. We lay at the Dumaine Street wharf, pier 33. Once the *Queen* was tied to the worn timberheads, the wheel slowed, stopped. The gulls settled watchfully back on the wharf boat roof. We had arrived. We felt so good about it that it was almost as if we, the passengers, had personally navigated the big steamer down a dangerous river and had brought her safely to the great goal of all the steamboats of the past, the remarkable port of New Orleans.

There is no other city in the world quite like New Orleans. It is not French nor is it Spanish nor Italian nor really American, either, but a subtle mixture of all four, with a blend of Mississippi River water thrown in, which is one of the secret ingredients in the recipe. New Orleans may have begun as a French colony, but France had never taught her colonists what it was like to be at the mercy of a river like the Mississippi, yet enjoying its benefits. The people began to change as soon as they had been here for a while—speaking French, of course, following French ways, but changed by living in this wild, swamp-haunted lowland, along a huge and merciless river.

The French built New Orleans, but after the big fire of 1788 and the other in 1794, it was largely rebuilt by the Spanish, who had acquired Louisiana for a while. Most of the original French architecture was lost in the fires; that which was rebuilt had the galleries, the intricate wrought-iron railings, the hidden patios, the soft colors of pink, buff, yellow, blue and green which the Spanish admired in their houses. The river humidity quickly softened the colors still more, and the mold and moss which throve in such a damp atmosphere soon gave a look of age to the rebuilt city.

While Spain occupied New Orleans, there was a mingling of races, a mixture of French and Spanish through marriages, a blending with other European blood, producing the aristocratic Creoles, identified with that city. They were beautiful people who felt they could never be happy anywhere but in New Orleans.

What is called the Old French Quarter or the Vieux Carré is not really French, though I suppose it is more that than anything else: French with a Spanish accent in the wrought-iron balconies and old pink bricks, the little gardens with their damp stone flagging, a banana tree in a corner and a bougainvillea vine over the wall. The gardens lie at the end of narrow, dark passageways, leading in from the street and barred by an ornamental iron gate which keeps out strangers, but lets them look in wistfully at a bit of a forgotten way of life. But not forgotten here.

You cannot take one aspect of New Orleans and say, "This is New Orleans," because it is a complicated place. It is the little streets and the garden walls and the old brick house walls rising from the *banquettes* or sidewalks, which you need for that special recipe of the old city. There must be the atmosphere of the leisurely Old South itself, which has never died, and the Mississippi curving vastly around the city, and the smells of roasting coffee, the bananas coming in, and the ferry whistles squeaking all day and most of the night, and the scent of oleanders in Jackson Square. There must also be the width and traffic of Canal Street, the universities, the fine avenues and homes of the Garden District, and the parks, and the Dueling Oaks.

There must be the sour smell of the narrow back streets early in the morning, and the sounds of the gulls mewing over the river and lining up on the nearby roofs, and the deep-throated whistles of tankers, freighters and towboats, coming and going.

There must be the French Market on Friday, when the big supply of fish comes in and is sold—wet baskets of wriggling blue crabs from river and bayou and sea, and piles of shrimp, complete with all their whiskers, feelers, legs and black, staring eyes; and pompano and sea bass and carp and squid and swordfish and oysters, so that the smell all but makes you reel when you step into the fish market. But it is not as strong as it used to be before sanitation pushed in and made refrigeration, screenwire and cleanliness obligatory, even in that once casual and most odorous and fascinating place.

Outside, under the yellow-brown stucco portico, are neat piles of oranges and lemons, grapefruit and mandarins, and baskets of little kumquats, each fruit picked with a twig and glossy leaves for freshness and beauty; and prickly pears, fennel, guavas, red bananas, mangoes, Chinese plums and imported grapes. Gaudy souvenir shops filled with Mexican, Japanese and New Jersey junk occupy the place where old Choctaw women once sat silently under the ancient portico to sell filé and bay leaves. One of Jean Laffite's henchmen, Louis Chighizola, or Nez Coupé, had a stall here when his pirating days were over.

Not so long ago, there were Negro women selling hot rice cakes, called *callas*, and live chickens with their legs tied, ducks and geese, and great red and yellow festoons of violently hot peppers from the Cajun country, over near New Iberia.

At each end of the French Market there is a coffee shop, the Café du Monde and the Morning Call, where one of the first things to do, once off the boat, is to have a cup of Louisiana coffee with hot milk and three square, blistering-hot, powdered-sugared, holeless doughnuts, as a sort of initiation rite to New Orleans. Even children there take much-diluted coffee, heavily sugared in the New Orleans style; it is part of being in that old city, to follow the custom.

The powdered sugar will fluff on your coat or dress. The doughnuts may burn your tongue; the coffee may seem very strong if you have decided not to have it with milk; but it is all somehow special. Different!

The coffee is subtly bitter with chickory, as the New Orleanians like it—at any rate, most of them put so much sugar into their coffee that the bitterness is changed. But when you order it with hot milk at the coffee shops, it is fun to watch the cook pour hot coffee and hot milk at the same time, each from its own big steel pot with an extraordinarily long spout, aiming from each side and hitting the mug with just the right amounts of both and with never a drop splashed overboard.

The Café du Monde has a Paris-like sidewalk cafe across from Jackson Square, at the west end of the market. The Morning Call, very plain and not always very clean, is indoors at the east end of the market. Here, the enormous silver-plated sugar bowls are chained together along the old marble-topped counter.

The coffee shops are not really tourist features. New Orleans has always had them. It was a long time before the old city got around to putting forth an effort toward attracting tourists. At last, the city formed the Vieux Carré Association, to preserve, protect and maintain the French Quarter itself in its old authentic atmosphere. Under the ruthless advance of decay, modernizing, or indifference, it was rapidly being lost. The Association has worked hard to restore accurately and to maintain in the old atmosphere something of the real look of the French Quarter—always on the shabby side, outwardly, but inwardly elegant. The coffee shops themselves have probably changed little, except perhaps for higher sanitary standards imposed by modern New Orleans.

It was in certain other coffee shops that much quiet intrigue once took place. Plots of a dark and sinister nature were hatched over cups of potent black New Orleans coffee. But in the shops across from Jackson Square one had coffee and doughnuts after Mass on Sunday morning, or after the theater, or during Carnival, or at any time at all. That the tourists discovered the shops was purely coincidental, and I doubt if it mattered a great deal to the owners or to New Orleans.

23. *Ghosts of New Orleans*

One who knew the coffee shops well was the elegant
pirate, Jean Laffite, who disliked being called a pirate and
was known to have dueled and killed men who insisted on this
insult. For Jean Laffite, king of the wild swamps in the Barataria country, ruler of a kingdom of pirates and privateers
and a fleet of corsairs which were not above hijacking a slave
ship, killing the owners and crew, scuttling the vessel, and
taking the cargo back to Grande Isle to sell, nevertheless protested his innocence. In spite of what Governor Claibourne
called him, Laffite insisted that he was a gentleman, and if he
took ships, it was because they were Spanish vessels; he had
letters of marque from Colombia, giving him permission to do
so. Governor Claibourne was not impressed. Jean Laffite
and his gang were still pirates, so far as the governor was concerned. His problem was how to stop their activities and lock

them in the calaboose.

The brothers Laffite had a flare for drama. When placards were put up in New Orleans, advertising a reward of $500 for their capture, they casually sauntered up and read the words, smiled at the New Orleanians watching them in admiration, then walked off as blandly as if they were going to the coffee shop. The next day, all the Laffite posters had mysteriously vanished, and in their places were signs advertising a reward of $1,500, to be paid by Laffite for the capture of Governor Claibourne! The governor was not amused, but New Orleans loved it. The pirates out at Grande Isle, Chenière au Tigre and Barataria rocked with laughter. The nerve of that Laffite! What a man!

He was invited into the best homes, but very often when this happened the daughters of the family were not present. The man of the household had private business to discuss with Laffite and often contrived to get a bargain in African slaves just taken off a ship. So Jean Laffite walked with a confident gait through the city whose governor was determined to capture him.

When the British, during the War of 1812, headed toward the mouth of the Mississippi with the intention of taking Louisiana and making it part of the British Empire, the old city—old even then, for it had been built soon after Bienville and Iberville settled upon the spot in 1700—was in a panic. It had poor supplies of arms and few soldiers. It was open to attack not only up the more obvious highway of the Mississippi, but up the back way via Lake Borgne, the Rigolets Pass and Lake Pontchartrain, as well as through many bayous. A good many of the passable bayou routes from the Gulf traversed the Barataria country. And out there in those uncharted places where Laffite's booty was hidden in a dozen strategic spots, were more than a thousand men who were Laffite's pirates. They had plenty of guns, gunflints, ammunition and courage. But they were outlaws, and no one thought to ask them to come and help defend New Orleans, the city where placards offered rewards for the capture of their leader.

The Laffite brothers, Pierre and Jean, might have looked like upright citizens and might have entered the best homes, might have walked unscathed on the streets of the Vieux Carré, but a good many of their henchmen were not so well groomed, handsome and confident. Some were downright piratical in appearance and character. The Laffite lieutenants ranged from bluff, loyal old Dominique You, who had been an artillerist with Napoleon and could never forget his idol; to the sinister Johnny Gambi, who was finally killed by his own men. There was tall, dark René Beluche; he, also, had fought with Napoleon, and after his wild life as a buccaneer along the Barataria coast, he looked too much like a genuine storybook pirate for anyone to confuse him with anything else. People feared Beluche and Louis Chighizola, too, partly because they looked so terrible. Louis had been a wild youth and had lost part of his nose in a sword fight. He was called Nez Coupé—Cut Nose—and people shuddered to see him, the pirate with his scars and his gold ring in one ear lobe, part of his nose gone and a ruthless look in his eyes.

When the British were coming up the back ways and bayous—and up the Mississippi itself—to attack and take New Orleans, and then to burn it, so they vowed, General Andrew Jackson came hastily to defend the city. He had brought several thousand of his Indian-fighting, squirrel-rifle soldiers, men out of the hills and backwoods of Tennessee and Kentucky. They were sure shots and deadly when they fought in the forests and swamps, which was what they were going to have to do to keep the British away from New Orleans. They had their own flintlocks, but were short of flints to fire them.

Andrew Jackson received word from Jean Laffite, still out at Barataria and itching to get into the fight, that if he were pardoned and removed from the list of outlaws to be taken on sight, he would bring a thousand men and all the guns, flints, and ammunition Jackson would need. But he must come as a free man, a good American, to be able to defend his beloved country.

That made Governor Claibourne writhe. To have this hated outlaw, this pirate, this—this—unspeakable wretch who had publicly made fun of him, the governor . . . but if New Orleans were to continue to exist, perhaps . . . well, he might consider it. . . .

And out of the remote swamps of the Barataria country and the hidden places known only to outlaws, came a motley crew . . . the pirates and privateers and bandits and cutthroats. They came trooping up the river roads, came by pirogue and canoe and keelboat, flocking into New Orleans, making free with the place which had once put a price on their heads. A good many of them still looked like pirates— swarthy black beards, scarred faces, earrings flashing, swords and cutlasses thrust in sashes. Oh, they were a wonderful sight, and many a boy in New Orleans never forgot what he saw from the gallery before his frightened mama hurried him indoors and closed the shutters.

It was Laffite and his gang, along with the flints and guns and ammunition they contributed to the cause, that helped Andrew Jackson save New Orleans. The Americans suffered a loss of less than a dozen men, while the British lost seven hundred dead.

After the battle, Laffite and his followers separated. Some of them reformed; others went to more fertile fields of pirating. Beluche went down to South America, where he commanded a ship and became part of the history of Venezuela. Johnny

Gambi went back to pirating until his men cut his throat. Dominique You reformed and went into New Orleans politics. The Laffites vanished.

In 1821, the latter were known to have built a colony down on Galveston Bay, where Laffite's old business was resumed. When he was ordered to clear out, by the commander of ships sent from the United States Government, he begged the space of one night. . . . When morning came at last, the colony was in ruins, and Jean Laffite and all his men had disappeared. No one ever heard of them again, or of their whereabouts. Knowing Jean Laffite, it is to be doubted that he left off pirating forever. He undoubtedly proceeded with his business somewhere along the Mexican coast, or in South America, where René Beluche had gone. Who knows? But we do know that, down in the Barataria country, on a mound above Barataria Bayou and the marshes, there is a little ceme-

tery which has a whitewashed tomb indicating that Jean
Laffite lies within. But no one knows for certain, even now,
about Laffite, the slippery one.

New Orleans is still strongly flavored with the past, and
the past cannot forget the gaudy characters of the pirates who
came in by trail and bayou to save New Orleans from the
British, nor forget the well-dressed, handsome, always-excit-
ing, mysterious Jean Laffite. His ghost still walks New Orleans streets when fog off the river hangs in blurred globes
around street lamps, and the little back ways of the Vieux
Carré are misty and secretive.

To recapture some of this unforgotten past in New Orleans,
the best way to have come is by steamboat, that old-time
conveyance which is almost lost today. To get off a steamboat in the early morning hours, and to walk the old streets
of the ancient city, is a perfect way to find some of the
stories of its past.

I was awake early the morning after our arrival in New
Orleans. There was a considerable amount of commotion
going on outside, chains clanking, men shouting in a foreign
tongue, sounds of bumping, a petulant tooting of tug whistles
and a clamor of gulls disturbed over something.

Hastily dressing, then walking to the stern, I could see that
the Japanese freighter, the *Takai Maru*, was preparing to
leave. The Japanese captain, immaculate and crisp in his dark
blue serge uniform, white cap and beautiful white gloves with
buttons at the wrists, imperiously directed his Oriental crew
in casting off. The New Orleans dock crew did its part below
on the splintery wharf.

Watching with me were some of our own people. Our
young first mate, who first came on the river in 1953 as a
calliope player on the steamer *Avalon*, even before he was
out of college, observed the imperious way in which the

Japanese officer operated. He snapped out his commands shrilly, with a sizzle and a no-nonsense arrogance.

"We wouldn't have any crew left if *we* carried on like that," mused Doc Hawley, "but I guess the Orientals are used to it."

"That's the way the Japanese commanders ordered their men about during the war," commented a passenger wryly, "and *they* got results! But look where it landed them!"

The freighter captain was getting results, too. He wasn't at all steamed up about it, simply gave his sharp orders, waved his white gloves in emphasis. And the *Takai Maru* moved smoothly away from her berth, the accompanying tugs fastened alongside, guiding the big vessel out into the Mississippi. There she turned in a great curve to head downstream and out to sea.

We watched, there on the stern of the *Delta Queen's* texas deck, with her old-fashioned, algae-scummed, mud-stained, red and white wheel motionless below us. We waved at the white-gloved captain, who turned crisply on his heel and did not wave back.

The gloves were what the first mate couldn't stop thinking about.

"I'd like to see white gloves on some of us here on the *Delta Queen!* Bet they wouldn't stay white for long!"

In the early morning mists, I went off the landing stage and into the long, dark wharf shed, filled to the ceiling in some places with large burlap bags from South America, crates containing something mysteriously pungent, great boxes covering half a block of space, all waiting to be loaded on some incoming ship.

The floor of the wharf shed was a soft and resilient thing, oiled wood blocks on which footsteps were muffled. I found my way out of the long, dusky structure and into the misty morning light of a foggy dawn in New Orleans. I emerged exactly opposite historic Jackson Square, with General Andrew Jackson himself waving his hat above the palm trees. There was no sign of Jean Laffite, but I suspected he was somewhere about, too!

Once across the street from the waterfront buildings and the brewery, I was immediately in a different world, the world of the Vieux Carré and the past. The east and west tiers of the elegant Pontalba apartments lay on either side of Jackson Square. Their intricate wrought-iron railings bore the monogram AP entwined—Almonester-Pontalba—signifying something of what the Almonester and Pontalba families did for old New Orleans. It was they who had such a large part in the rebuilding the Vieux Carré after the great fires. Old Don Andres Almonester y Roxas was considered New Orleans' chief benefactor; for years the prayer in convent and cathedral was "God be thanked for Almonester!"

He built St. Louis Cathedral after the first one burned in the fire of 1788, built the Cabildo and the Presbytère on either side of the dignified cathedral, to give it balance and greater meaning, filling the entire block. The Cabildo and the Presbytère used to be the administrative buildings of city and church, but now they are museums filled with the story of old New Orleans, and with the natural history of Louisiana and the history of its people. Don Andres built a hospital, too, as well as performing many other good deeds of charity. It was no wonder New Orleans revered him.

The Cathedral, Presbytère and Cabildo are to the north of Jackson Square, the two sets of Pontalba apartments flanking it on east and west, while the river, wharves and French Market are on the south—or as close to these points of the compass as a city built on a curve of the Mississippi can become. The streets radiate from the river in so many directions that it is almost impossible to know in just which direction they do go—or to find your way back after a rambling walk.

Jackson Square was almost deserted early in the morning, except for the pigeons and a fluttering of small birds in the camphor trees. The banana tree across from the Pontalba apartments on the west had a large, dangling purple bud, ready to bloom for many days and to produce, incredibly, a real, full-sized bunch of bananas by late summer. The dove trees were in bloom, the tropical Davidias, natives of the South Pacific. Their pink-purple, four-inch flowers, artistically blotched with dark red-purple, looked very much like Hawaiian orchids arranged on long, bending boughs.

The beds of white crinum lilies around General Jackson's statue were battered after the recent rains, but the flowers were still fragrant. The palm trees rattled their fronds a little, showering down a brief flurry of dewdrops which, one by one, ran along the furrows of the big leaves. A big gray pigeon flew up from where an old man on a bench had been feeding it, and sat on top of the dignified head of General Jackson. Astride his horse, which is perpetually rearing in an improbable attitude on a granite pedestal in the middle of the Square, the general seems to be tirelessly acknowledging the acclaim of the city which he saved from the British in 1815.

Jackson Square was called the Place d'Armes during the time of the French and Spanish, the place where soldiers drilled, where public announcements were made and whippings and executions took place, and where the flag flew. It was here that the French flag waved until it was pulled down and the Spanish flag put up, and where again the French banner waved, until the grief-stricken day when it must go down forever and the American Stars and Stripes fly in its place. The name of the Place d'Armes was changed when New Orleans, with some reluctance but with a good deal of genuine gratitude, owed its existence to rough old Andy Jackson and his Tennessee squirrel-hunters, who had beaten the British army in the Louisiana cypress swamps along the river.

The square was filled with memories . . . memories of Carnival and with the desperate events of the War Between the States . . . of the terrible day when Admiral Farragut's ships came up the Mississippi, after fighting their way past the lower forts, to take over New Orleans . . . of old, fine days when the Pontalba apartments were the most sought-after homes in New Orleans. Upstairs in one of them, now part of the Louisiana State Museum, apartments are furnished as they once were, with marble vases of great size, a bust of Napoleon, velvet drapes at floor-length windows, canopied beds and an old French slipper-shaped tub for baths.

The pigeon had no proper respect, or else felt friendly. It sat on the general's head and cooed loudly. Two sparrows vied snappily for a perch on his upraised hat. In the trees, dozens of Tennessee warblers were singing and flitting, appropriately enough, near the man from their namesake state. Perhaps they had come up the curve of Mexico and landed here at last, or had flown over the vast waters of the Gulf of Mexico and up the Mississippi in the night. They would stop here for a while and then work their way up the Mississippi Flyway, would reach Tennessee within two weeks, and mid-Illinois in early May, and Wisconsin in mid-May. I would follow them for thirteen hundred miles, and still they would continue, singing all the way up to Canada to nest.

It was too early for the museums to be open, but the whole Vieux Carré is a museum, so locked doors didn't matter. To be seen inside, however, would be the cell in the old calaboose which once briefly held Jean Laffite. There is an ironclad submarine which the Confederates used in the war; and costumes from former Carnival kings and queens, as well as portraits of effeminate men and unreal-looking women, people of the past who once lived and had their being along these streets and in the shuttered houses of the Vieux Carré. There would be exhibits and dioramas of birds of Louisiana, and the paintings made by John James Audubon of those same birds, many of them painted during his stay in New Orleans itself.

Upstairs in the Cabildo there is something else, a thing which reposed voiceless in a glass and ebony case, there in the cool gloom of early morning: the death mask of Napoleon Bonaparte.

Napoleon had known of New Orleans, although he had never come there. It had been the chief city in the French colony in America, after Quebec and Montreal became Canadian. He had professed to be fond of New Orleans and of the Louisiana people, yet he had betrayed them when he sold the Louisiana Territory to the United States for fifteen million dollars, in 1803. But Napoleon had defended his act: he had needed the money to pursue his current war and maintain the honor of France. Yet he had lost everything, finally, and had languished on the island of St. Helena, exiled forever.

There were many who said it was a good thing; let the tyrant stay where he was, and good riddance. But the Bonapartists, many of whom were full of violent partisanship in the distant colony of France which New Orleans still considered itself, plotted as to how they could rescue their emperor and bring him to America. If the French themselves were satisfied to leave him shamefully in exile, then his loyal people in the New World would welcome him. What Napoleon Bonaparte, given his health for another decade, might have done to change the history of America, was fortunately never to be known.

Night after night, in the shuttered secrecy of certain houses in the Vieux Carré, in the Absinthe House and the upstairs rooms of Maspero's Exchange, plans went quietly forward. A schooner, the *Seraphine,* was purchased with funds raised by the Creole Bonapartists. And one of the ablest seamen in New Orleans was hired to take the ship to St. Helena and rescue the emperor.

Not any man could accomplish a tricky piece of work like this, but a pirate might, someone like Dominique You, who had had so many years of plain and fancy pirating and seamanship with his superior, Jean Laffite. Dominique You had reformed, had become a respected citizen, but he still thrilled to the opportunity to sail again, and to perform a daring feat of the riskiest pirating of all—stealing an emperor!

The *Seraphine* was ready. A picked crew of tough Barataria men was hired. A house at 500 Chartres Street was presented and made ready for the coming of Napoleon. When Dominique You thought of it, he could have wept with sentimental affection, that his beloved hero, under whom he had fought at Austerlitz and Jena, was really coming here to Louisiana, and under his own watchful care.

And then the invincible Napoleon Bonaparte, emperor of the French and one-time dictator who hoped to conquer the world, died on his island in the South Atlantic.

Napoleon lay dead, and Dominique You was crushed. The *Seraphine* was of no use now in rescuing an emperor. It lay empty at the wharf where the Mississippi curved around New Orleans, forever leading to the sea. The Barataria men were disappointed, too. This would have been a supreme adventure, something even Laffite had never accomplished, and now it was too late. The house at the corner of Chartres Street was put to other uses, though it still stands and is still known as the Napoleon House.

But if the emperor himself could not come to New Orleans, a part of himself could. His personal physician had made a plaster cast of the emperor's face after death. He took this mask to France where, years later, three bronze castings were made. Two remained in Paris, but the third was brought by Doctor Antommarchi himself to New Orleans where, in a very special ceremony, he presented it to the city.

The mask reposed in the Cabildo for years without any protection or care, aside from an occasional dusting. In the War Between the States, when General Butler's Federals overran New Orleans during the Occupation, and stole and desecrated many southern treasures, someone made off with the priceless death mask of Napoleon Bonaparte.

No one knew where it was until, suddenly, much later, the city treasurer himself, so the story goes, observed a passing junk wagon, on top of whose load of debris reposed the calm, unseeing face of Napoleon of France. Getting hold of his composure, he hastily bought the precious relic from the junkman. He kept it safely at home for thirty years, then finally restored it to the Cabildo.

And again it was stolen. But it was quickly recovered, and, this time, it was placed in a plate glass case, on a marble pedestal. And perhaps of all the pieces of the past up there in the museum, that arresting, cryptic mask of the man who wanted to conquer the world, the man who sold Louisiana to America, the emperor whom the pirates were going to rescue from exile, when death did the rescuing, is one of the most fascinating and meaningful.

Pirate's Alley passes back of the Cabildo and the Cathedral. It may have known pirates, just as most of the other narrow streets of New Orleans did, but the name remains, at least. That spring day, a few artists were bringing out their paintings for the spring exhibition held in connection with Spring Fiesta in New Orleans. Spring Fiesta follows Easter and is a gentler, more cultural celebration than Carnival, which precedes Lent. The artists along Pirate's Alley were complaining of the damp weather and of how it was making their water-color paintings curl. Oils and watercolors were hung on the iron fence outside the Cathedral garden and along Jackson Square's fence, too. The little narrow alley with its big, gray, paving slates was already growing cluttered with easels and stools and artists and a few casual spectators. Even so early, a sidewalk artist was making a crayon portrait of a young visitor.

From the back door of a shop came the smell of boiling brown sugar, to announce a new batch of pecan pralines for the day's tourists. Nearby was the shabby old Absinthe House, where some of the Napoleon plot took place and where, stories go, Andrew Jackson met with Jean Laffite to plan the Battle of New Orleans, though there are several other spots which claim this honor. There was the Napoleon House itself, still on its dingy corner, and the Beauregard House, and Madame John's Legacy in the old French style, and the place where Paul Morphy, chess wizard, lived.

There was the ancient and unadorned facade of Antoine's restaurant, which no doubt has changed very little since it was begun by the Alciatore family in 1840. Certainly the old rooms, the plain white china and silver and chairs, the walls covered with pictures and letters from celebrities who have dined here on *Pompano en Papillote*, *Les Huîtres en Coquille à la Rockefeller*, *Les Escargots Farcis*, and *Pomme de Terre Soufflées*, must look much the same.

Morning was growing, shops were opening, crowds were coming. Midmorning unaccountably was here and so were the people, and the ghosts of the past had flitted away. Pirate's Alley was jammed. Jackson Square was swarming with children, brought in buses on an excursion from Shreveport and Natchitoches. The coffee shops were filled. Traffic was heavy.

The Old French Quarter had lost some of its mysterious atmosphere of early morning in the matter-of-factness of today.

There are many other fascinating things to see in New Orleans; the French Quarter is only a small part of it. There are the long, elegant avenues where the big homes are, and the universities and convents and other seats of learning; the parks, the zoo, the lakes; the areas of all new, ranch-type homes of extreme modern style and splendor, and the beaches along Lake Pontchartrain, now New Orleans's second coast. There are the old cemeteries and the amazing burying ground which is Metairie Cemetery, with all the tombs raised above ground because of the sogginess of the earth and the presence of water leaking in from the nearby Mississippi. There are the old plantations, the battlegrounds, the modern airports, the miles of small, new homes in the endless developments engulfing what not long ago was alligator-infested swamp land around New Orleans.

But it all hinges on the river, always the river, leading New Orleans boats one hundred and twenty miles down to the sea, leading them eighteen hundred miles northward to the head of navigation in Minnesota. No matter what else might come to it, or what it might become, New Orleans would always be governed by the river and by the boats coming to its port.

Back in the quiet of the *Delta Queen*, I walked to the river side of the deck and watched a flock of dark-headed gulls clamoring and diving for scraps tossed out by the cooks. The big empty space where the *Takai Maru* and her white-gloved captain had so lately stood, was still open, waiting for another ship. Far around the curve of the river, the sunshine lit the freighters and tankers, as far as I could see down the Mississippi as it bent and narrowed toward its ultimate union with the sea. And even as it poured out into the Gulf of Mexico, far into the salt water, the thick brown fluid of the Mississippi would be distinct, not mingling at once with the ocean, but holding its identity, a river in the sea.

It was Monday afternoon, and the time for departure drew near. Food supplies were brought aboard. The bell rang and the visitors went ashore, lines were cast off, and the *Delta Queen* moved away from the Dumaine Street dock. Quiet and lovely on the river, moving placidly yet powerfully against the current, the steamer paddled easily, as if glad to be on her way again. She would travel rapidly until, near Baton Rouge, she began to climb the slope, would buck that big spring current coming down from Minnesota and the Alleghenies and the Wisconsin and the Missouri and the Illinois.

And as she paddled on her way, the triumphant ghosts of all the long-gone steamboats which made the Mississippi a two-way river blew their spectral whistles and clanged their silent bells. The *Delta Queen*, last of a long line and far from being ready to join her ancestors in oblivion, proudly navigated northward, as the *Natchez* and the *Robert E. Lee* had done nearly a hundred years before. Paddle wheel digging deeply in the brown and muddy water of the Mississippi, bucket planks throwing spray into the sunset, she was on her way, gloriously homeward bound.

Index

VIRGINIA S. EIFERT

feels that her roster of books about the Mississippi River would not be complete without the story of the *Delta Queen*, last of the overnight, stern-wheel, passenger steamboats on Mark Twain's tremendous river.

Mrs. Eifert, who knows the Mississippi so thoroughly and enthusiastically, both from the standpoint of its natural history and its human history, was especially well suited to write this engrossing story of the *Delta Queen* and the Steamboat Era. She has traveled 4000 miles on the *Delta Queen* to obtain firsthand material. The resulting book has a fresh approach which the reader also feels in her *Mississippi Calling* and *River World*. It is the same sensitive interpretive quality that is to be found in her five books about Abraham Lincoln.

Mrs. Eifert is editor of *The Living Museum* magazine and author of nature books for the Illinois State Museum. She frequently teaches nature courses at *The Clearing*, in northern Wisconsin.